Teach Your Wife How to Be a Widow

Teach Your Wife How to Be a Widow

Joseph Newman—Directing Editor

U.S.NEWS & WORLD REPORT BOOKS

A division of U.S.News & World Report, Inc.

WASHINGTON, D.C.

Contents

Appendix

Illustrations

Acknowledgments

The editors of *U.S.News & World Report Books* have been assisted by a number of specialists in preparing this book. They are indebted to Margaret Daly for her work in researching and writing the manuscript; Martin L. Kamerow, C.P.A., for material on tax matters; Elizabeth Fagg Olds, who edited the manuscript; and Roslyn Grant, who coordinated the editorial work and kept the book up-to-date.

Valuable assistance was also received from the American Bankers Association, American Bar Association, Associated Credit Bureaus of America, Inc., Bureau of Labor Statistics, Census Bureau, Chase Manhattan Bank, Federal Housing Administration, Federal Trade Commission, Health Insurance Institute, Institute of Life Insurance, Insurance Information Institute, Internal Revenue Service, Mortgage Bankers Association of America, National Association of Investment Clubs, National Association of Mutual Savings Banks, National Better Business Bureaus, National Home Improvement Council, National Selected Morticians, New York Bar Association, New York Stock Exchange, Office of Interstate Land Sales (HUD), Over-the-Counter Information Bureau, Riggs National Bank, Shareholders Management Company, Social Security Administration, U.S. Savings Bonds Division of the Treasury, United Student Aid Funds, and the Veterans Administration.

CHAPTER 1

Thinking
the
Unthinkable

Is your wife prepared to be a widow?

It is a question no man likes to contemplate. After all, the thought of your wife's widowhood inevitably evokes awareness of your own mortality. And who wants to think about his own demise?

Yet, both you and your wife might give the matter careful consideration. In this age of high speed on the highways and high pressure in the office, her preparation for widowhood could be put to the test without a moment's notice. Consider this case, for example. An airplane crashed near a large midwestern city not long ago. The flight was a "businessman's special," and all passengers were killed. What happened to four women widowed by this tragic flight was not unlike the fate of many others who become widows unexpectedly, or even with forewarning:

Four
new widows
face
problems

• Jane, aged thirty-two, was left with two small children. Her husband, Jack, had just changed jobs. Celebrating a sizable pay increase, they had bought a new house, and most of their savings and investments went into the down payment.

In the hustle of learning his new job, Jack had failed to straighten out his personal finances. He had not purchased insurance to cover the mortgage. Nor had he followed through on personal life insurance plans—even though he was not yet eligible for group life insurance through his new employer.

Jane found herself in severe trouble: two small children; a $300-a-month mortgage to pay off; little savings; no nest egg from insurance; no job skills, since she had never worked; only about $450 from Social Security benefits coming in each month. Even though she found a job, the pay was limited, and much of it went to babysitters while she worked. The future did not look promising. . . .

• Katherine was in her fifties, her children grown. Her husband, John, left $60,000 in insurance. They recently had sold their house and moved to an apartment, investing some of the profits of the sale in corporate bonds and common stock, and placing the rest in a savings account. Together, these resources provided an income of about $3,000 a year.

When Katherine received the $60,000 insurance money, she deposited it in a savings account paying 5 percent a year. That gave her another $3,000 annually. And that was all. Too young to collect even reduced Social Security benefits, she received only

airlines settlement?

$6,000 a year income—before taxes—from securities and savings. After paying $250 a month in rent, she had only $250 for all other expenses, including taxes.

That was enough for survival, but the income hardly provided for the modestly comfortable life Katherine was accustomed to. Realizing that she had to manage her nest egg to gain more income, she remembered how John had talked about the exciting investment potentials of common stocks and how a smart investor could have "tripled his money" in the market over the past few years.

Unfortunately, John imparted only that attitude, without much knowledge or caution to go along with the fantasy. As a result, when John's brother raved about a "sure thing" coming up in the stock market, Katherine immediately withdrew $10,000 from her savings and invested in the stock. Six months later, the company collapsed and the stock became virtually worthless. Not only had Katherine lost considerable capital, but her income-producing nest egg had also been reduced, and she was forced eventually to sell some securities just to pay everyday bills. . . .

• Mary, aged forty-eight, had a son who required one more year to complete his college education, and a daughter entering college that fall. The youngest child was twelve.

Aside from a sum of insurance money, the most substantial asset Mary's husband left was a parcel of undeveloped shorefront property in Maine. He had purchased the acreage for about $7,000 several years ago, and it was now worth more than $20,000, with every promise of continuing to rise in value.

Mary had worked as an executive secretary before marriage, and she found a job immediately to

help pay the bills now that her husband's income
had ceased. Her two older children also worked
part time; survivors' benefits from Social Security
coverage rounded out the family income.

The financial picture was not bad. There were
some minor annoyances, such as the fact that Mary
could not obtain a charge account at a local department store—even though she was working full
time, earning a respectable salary. The main problems were college tuition for the older children, and
summer camp for the youngest.

The older youngsters were able to arrange low-
cost student loans. Still, Mary realized she would
need an additional $5,000 or $6,000 to cover costs
for the next couple of years. The simplest solution
seemed to be to sell part of the Maine land. She had
never paid much attention to that investment anyway. It was her husband's venture, and she had
been surprised to learn when his estate was settled
that the land was worth so much.

Mary sold a third of the land, for $8,000, thus
giving up part of a valuable asset in order to get
ready cash. The parcel did continue to appreciate
rapidly in worth after the sale. In simple fact, Mary
could have held on to the land and used it as collateral for a loan—easily repaid from her salary—
had she known that she had that option. . . .

• Virginia was sixty-two when her husband died
in the crash. Her financial situation seemed solid—
quite a bit of insurance, the house paid for, and reduced widow's benefits from Social Security. But
she was not accustomed to taking care of the house
herself. When a roof repairman rang her door bell
and offered to patch her roof because he "could see
it was falling apart," she panicked and told him to
go ahead, even though the cost would be $800 in

cash. There was nothing really wrong with the roof. The "repair" job rapidly deteriorated. And Virginia was out $800.

She faced another needless problem, too. Her husband had purchased a new car in anticipation of some retirement travel. The car was financed through a dealer, and payments were $150 a month. Since there had been no reason to notify the dealer of her husband's death—or so Virginia thought— she diligently paid off the entire loan in monthly installments, not realizing that the contract included credit life insurance. When her husband died, the loan would have automatically been paid in full—if Virginia had notified the right people. Her husband simply had not told her about the arrangement. . . .

Virginia was not a stupid woman, nor particularly naive. Like Katherine and Mary, she simply was inexperienced in many matters that befall widows. Jane, too, lacked such experience, and she faced the added financial burden left by her husband.

They lacked the necessary preparation

In each case, there had been insufficient communication between husband and wife about finances and widowhood. The three older women actually knew quite a bit about their family's cash flow situation and most of their important assets. Katherine and Mary did all the check-writing, and Mary's husband had consulted her whenever he purchased securities or insurance. But none of the husband-and-wife teams really had sat down to discuss financial management in detail, or to explore the many problems that would arise if the husband died.

How U.S. Life Spans Compare With Others

Examples of years of life expectancy at birth

	Male	Female
Sweden	71.9	76.5
Norway	71.0	76.0
Netherlands	70.7	76.5
Denmark	70.7	75.6
Israel	69.6	73.0
East Germany	69.2	74.4
Japan	69.1	74.3
Canada	68.8	75.2
Bulgaria	68.8	72.7
Switzerland	68.7	74.1
England and Wales	68.6	74.9
Ireland	68.1	71.9
Australia	67.9	74.2
Italy	67.9	73.4
Belgium	67.7	73.5
France	67.6	75.3
West Germany	67.6	73.6
Greece	67.5	70.7
Czechoslovakia	67.3	73.6
Spain	67.3	71.9
UNITED STATES	67.1	74.6
Scotland	66.9	73.1
Poland	66.9	72.8
Austria	66.3	73.5
U.S.S.R.	65.0	74.0

Source: United Nations

These are questions every family must face:

How will your family get along when you are gone? Can your wife take charge of your affairs and handle finances so that her life will continue in a relatively normal manner, without undue worry or strain? Will she be easy prey for bad advice or unscrupulous maneuvers? How about your children? Will they receive all the benefits you want for them?

How long will your wife be a widow? Will there be enough to live on for all those years?

Many women outlive their husbands

Statistics show that the average wife can expect close to ten years of widowhood. Typically, husbands are four years older than their wives, and

7 now (1992)

women outlive men by about five years. To figure
your particular situation by the averages, take the
difference in your ages, and add five years. If you
are fifty-five and she is forty-eight, the odds are
that she will be a widow for at least twelve years
(fifty-five minus forty-eight, plus five). If you are
sixty-three and she is sixty, count on eight years
for her to be on her own.

Remember, these are *average* expectations only.
In reality, many older women live well beyond the
deaths of their husbands. And if you are in your
thirties or forties, it seems likely that your wife will
be alive much longer than a decade or so more,
should you meet with an early death.

To most young and middle-aged Americans especially, death and widowhood do not seem likely at
all. This attitude prevails even though more young
people are killed by highway accidents and more
middle-aged men are felled by heart attack in the
United States than in any other country. Most
younger men think, "It can't happen to me." As a
result, they give only the most casual consideration
to the fate of the wife and youngsters if the husband suddenly isn't around anymore. Even many
older men, who presumably have faced the inevit-
ability of death more realistically, fail to teach
their wives how to get along as widows.

That's not to say that millions of women do not
manage very well, widowed or not. On the contrary,
more and more women are proving their ability to
handle their lives productively and shrewdly, without having to rely upon a male breadwinner. We
read of women serving on the boards of stock exchanges, female executives commanding salaries in
ranges traditionally reserved for men, young house-
wives organizing and running thriving businesses,

divorcees refusing alimony because they prefer to pay their own way.

In 1970, according to the United States Census Bureau, wives earned more than their husbands in 3.2 million families—7.4 percent of all husband-wife families in the U.S. The report also concluded that the trend was growing; in more and more families, the wife is the chief breadwinner.

According to federal government figures, working women brought home $131 billion in wages during a recent year. It has also been estimated that women collected $5 billion in insurance death benefits in one year. About $172 billion worth of stock and $10 billion in mutual funds have been registered in women's names. Women investors are not "just lucky." For instance, a study conducted at the University of Oklahoma tested women against men in managing an investment portfolio. Seventy-two percent of the women did better than the Dow Jones industrial averages, while only 33 percent of the men outperformed the Dow in the experiment. In fact, many women show their interest in finance by subscribing to publications traditionally thought to be for men only.

Whether a breadwinner or not, or a student of finance or not, the wife in many families all along has been the money manager, engineering and executing the family budget, making significant buying decisions, deciding how much goes into savings and how much into spending, even preparing the family tax return.

Certainly the expertise with which many women run their working lives and their family lives suggests that other women could be quite capable along the same lines. However, too many are ill-prepared. Either they have no experience with money matters or prefer to remain ignorant about them; or their husbands choose for whatever reasons not to share their own knowledge with their wives.

Even if your mate is one of the almost 40 million American women in the work force these days, she may know very little about financial management. Often the woman's wages are pooled with those of her husband under the latter's management, or she uses part or all of her earnings for a few special purposes. Perhaps her salary helps pay for her clothes and family entertainment. Perhaps it is being saved for college tuition for the children, for vacations, or for an addition to the house.

Can your wife manage money?

The question you must ask—and answer honestly—is, how much is your wife *really* involved in the overall financial operation of your life together? Have you given her the responsibility of financial management which most men learn as a matter of course in their working lives and as heads of households? Those are precisely the tools your wife will need to manage on her own.

If your wife already is a good business partner in your family's money management, there may be much in this book that she already knows. If she is not yet as involved as she should be, then there is a broad new field for her to master.

Never before have such skills been so necessary for a widow. The changing world has altered economic and social structures so that most widows face a tougher, more complicated life than in the past.

This generation is accustomed to living well, for instance; but inflation sees to it that the cost of the good life comes high. Better education increases our

demands. Improved health care produces a longer
life span, and extends the years to be provided for.
Modern health care also can mean prolonged, costly
terminal illnesses which can wipe out a husband's
hard-earned assets. National averages show that
many women complete their child-bearing by age
twenty-six. Thus, there can be a long span of
widowed years without Social Security, since benefits stop between the time the last child has grown
and the widow reaches age sixty or sixty-two.

And the closely-knit family whom the widow
once fell back upon has virtually disappeared.
Formerly, relatives often saw to the welfare of
widows. Now, in most cases, only the husband's
planning and the wife's financial know-how can
assure her security.

Some widows left destitute   To many wives, widowhood presents seemingly
insurmountable obstacles and horrifying responsi-
bilities—and at a time when they are least capable
of dealing with them.

A recent study by the Life Insurance Agency
Management Association and the Life Underwriter
Training Council examined the lives of 1,744
widows in the metropolitan areas of Boston, Chi-
cago, Houston, and San Francisco. Each woman's
husband had recently died before reaching age
sixty-five. The economic and psychological impact
of the husband's premature death was distressing:

• Nearly half the widows acknowledged that
handling family finances was difficult because their
husbands always had taken care of money matters.

• Less than one widow in every five said she had
ever discussed with her husband what should be
done with the life insurance proceeds if he died.

The Increase in One-Parent Families

Families Headed by Mothers Alone

	1965	1974	Change
Widows	2,301,000	2,505,000	Up 9%
Divorced, separated females	1,731,000	3,445,000	Up 99%
Single females	397,000	854,000	Up 115%

Families Headed by Fathers Alone

	1965	1974	Change
Widowers	443,000	407,000	Down 8%
Divorced, separated males	208,000	528,000	Up 154%
Single males	426,000	503,000	Up 18%

Note: The "single females" category has risen sharply as more unwed mothers have decided to keep their babies. Divorced fathers who have won custody of their children have caused the jump in the "divorced, separated males" category.

Source: U.S. Census Bureau

• Almost one in every three said that her family had no financial assets. Half had total assets of less than $1,000.

• Only 8 percent of the widows received as much as $25,000 from life insurance. The average was $9,150.

Nine thousand one-hundred fifty dollars! Less than $10,000. Even assuming there was also $1,000 or so in a savings account, plus (though not likely) a house free and clear, how far can $10,000 or $11,000 go these days? U.S. Department of Labor statistics showed that in late 1975 an income of at least $9,588 a year was required to maintain the most modest scale of living for a family of four. A "moderate" scale might be achieved on an annual budget of $15,318. And one that was "above average" required a budget of $22,294. Granted, those costs were for a hypothetical family of two adults and two youngsters. But it does not take much figuring to see the implications for your family, once you are gone.

Of course, you may be planning to leave much more of an estate than these modest sums. Perhaps you carry a significant amount of life insurance, own valuable securities, and have built a substantial equity in your home. Even if you do not have a major insurance program of your own, you probably are covered by some group insurance through your job.

But would your wife know what to do with $15,000, $25,000, or even $100,000 in insurance proceeds that suddenly became hers? According to the insurance companies, many widows spend their lump-sum insurance money within a year after receiving it.

Would your wife have to continue mortgage payments on your house month after month? Could she borrow money for the cost of your youngsters' schooling, if necessary? Does she know how to go about securing a substantial loan? Can she get one at all as a widow? Will she know how to make investments that insure income and preserve and expand capital as well?

It is ironic that many men work hard to "provide for the wife and kids" during their lifetime, yet do little, really, to safeguard the family welfare after the breadwinner is gone. They may have arranged their estates to the best possible advantage, yet failed to teach their wives how to live on their own. If this is your wife's need, you had better begin right now.

Start with the right attitude

It is not morbid for a man to spend years teaching his wife to be a widow. Seven out of ten husbands predecease their mates. Preparing your wife is therefore only sensible, and it is never too early to begin. But you must proceed in a tactful way.

For one thing, the subject matter is bound to be disturbing to her. (Before you grow impatient or upset yourself, do not overlook your own delay in approaching the topic because *you* did not want to face it straight on!)

For another thing, remember that much of what you will be talking about may be familiar ground for you, but confusing to your wife. You have been dealing with finances for a long time. Possibly she has not.

Rather than dwelling upon the thought of death, consider instead that your wife is learning to be self-sufficient—in case you have a prolonged illness or other incapacity. For that matter, much of the planning that you do together is really *life* planning. Getting your finances in order so you both know what to expect and what you can do with your resources should make the immediate future more enjoyable. And such planning also could contribute to shaping your retirement along lines you prefer. Thus, a positive attitude will make a difference.

You both also should be wary of the common assumption—sometimes unconscious—that women really cannot deal well with such matters. Statistics indicate that, even in grade school, boys usually outdo girls in mathematics. Some people think this derives from a natural male aptitude. However, many educators suspect the real reason is cultural: girls are raised to believe that mathematical sciences are not their province, and they cannot compete. So, they behave accordingly. This belief need not continue in your household.

Finally, remember that, as a teacher, you are helping your wife gain knowledge. And, knowledge *is* power. You will be gaining a business partner in your family financial life, possibly a strong and talented one. A true partner can relieve the burden of responsibility too many men shoulder alone. What is more, her growing competency can bring you peace of mind about your family's future.

Two major areas of education must be covered with your wife. One involves the way in which you have organized your estate; the other, how your wife will handle that estate after you are gone. In other words, how skilled a money manager will she be?

This book covers both aspects of family financial management. Indeed, they are very much intertwined. How wisely you have set up your estate dictates how much of an estate will be left for your wife to work with. On the other hand, knowing about general estate matters will not make much difference if she has not also acquired the techniques to manage her day-to-day finances in the framework of an overall plan for the coming years and even decades. As you talk together, keep in mind that there are lessons for you both to learn.

Your estate and the life it can bring Throughout this book are discussions of various ways to arrange your estate so it will be preserved and managed as nearly as possible in the manner you wish. Your wife should understand and discuss all choices and decisions with you, so she can take charge if necessary with minimum trouble and maximum effectiveness.

Before you go into detail about what assets you will be leaving, here are some preliminaries to think and talk about:

1. Both of you should realize that plans for a

widow's welfare vary with age. If a thirty-year-old man dies, his wife (providing she is also thirty) faces perhaps forty years of widowhood, possibly more. When a couple is aged sixty, the situation in some ways will probably be easier on the widow. She does not need to stretch the insurance money so far; usually the house is paid for; the children are grown and might offer her a home if necessary. She has different needs as a widow from those of the woman with a home to pay for, a family to raise, and a possible lifetime of loneliness in a husbandless future. (This does not mean that a sixty-year-old woman should not have a very good idea of what to expect; only that her problems are different.) Show your wife how your estate planning takes age factors into account, and let her help in such future planning.

2. Your wife should understand that there will probably be less money coming into the family coffers for her as a widow than as a wife. If you are earning $20,000 a year now, it would take a capital investment of $400,000, paying 5 percent annual interest, to yield the equivalent amount for her after you are gone. Most likely, that kind of income will not be possible. Maintaining $400,000 worth of life insurance, for instance, could cost a man of thirty-five $5,000 or more a year. That is a big bite out of any budget.

In any event, it is essential that your wife know exactly what money will be coming in after you die, and from what sources—Social Security, insurance, annuities, pension plans, rentals, and so forth.

3. Explore the possibility of your wife's having to work to supplement income when she is a widow. If she is already working and intends to keep on, fine. You both probably know the net gain from

her salary, in terms of the costs of her clothing, transportation, child care, and other expenditures.

If your wife must earn a salary after years of not working, she may face the problem of a tight job market. Teaching positions are harder to find these days, for instance. If she has to work for the first time, she may be confronted by even greater problems. As a worker without skills, she will find that many unskilled jobs bring in less than $100 a week. With small children and the necessity of paying someone to supervise them, that meager salary might leave virtually no cash at all. Consider planning now—perhaps through a part-time job or further education—for the possibility of her working in the future.

4. What about your widow's life style? Will it make sense for her to keep the house? Or will a smaller one do? What standard of living would she like to maintain? Will it be possible? What do both of you feel about college for your youngsters, even if money is scarce and they may not want to go?

5. Discuss where all your important papers are kept (see Chapter 11).

6. Make sure your wife meets and gets to know all the experts you use. Sit down together with your lawyer, your broker, your banker, and whoever else has significant dealings with your money.

Handling daily finances   Here's where you can be a teacher rather than a lecturer. Let your wife take over several family business matters she does not yet handle. If you do not already have a joint checking account, get one, and let her pay all the bills. In any case, let her make many of the decisions about what to pay and when, instead of merely following your suggestions. Let

College Expenses Climbing

Over a six-year span, basic costs will have risen an estimated 62 percent at private schools, 63 percent at public colleges. Costs at many colleges run far higher than average. The figures do not include expenses of books, clothing, transportation, and other items that can add $500 a year or more to the cost of college.

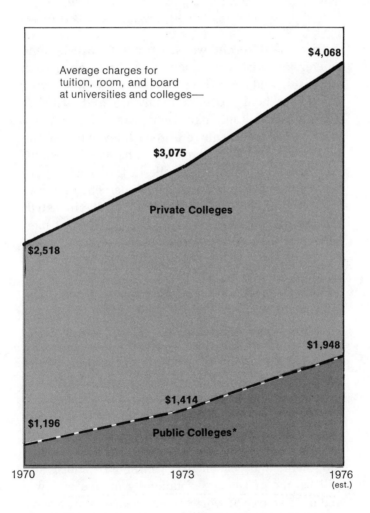

Average charges for tuition, room, and board at universities and colleges—

$4,068

$3,075

Private Colleges

$2,518

$1,948

$1,414

$1,196

Public Colleges*

1970   1973   1976
                              (est.)

*For state and local residents; tuition higher for out-of-state residents.

Source: U.S. Office of Education

her figure out the household cash flow and how best to balance the budget. Show her what records must be kept for your income tax returns. Have her set up a system for filing those records. When the time comes to prepare your return this year, share the task with her, or ask her to take a crack at it alone first.

In these different ways, your wife will become conversant with your business, your income, your expenses, and your investments, as well as with such household costs as insurance and utilities. Through the simple expedient of sharing responsibility, she will acquire a good knowledge of the business world. In a short time she may be asking why you allow $600 to lie idle in the checking account when it could be earning 5 percent in a savings account or even more if shrewdly invested. Women often have a penchant for details that men seldom possess. Once your wife has been bitten by the finance bug, she could become the best business partner you ever had.

Your reward will be many-sided. You will have a financially well-run household. You will gain freedom from handling the bills, checks, and tax records. Most important, you will know your wife can manage herself and your family alone if the need arises. You will know that if she should come into a large sum of money—say the payment of your insurance policy—she will not be stampeded into squandering it but will use the money wisely, exercising experienced business acumen, sound judgment, and seasoned reasoning. In short, she will be one of the few financially secure widows, and not a source of worry to her relatives or, worse, a charge of the community.

CHAPTER 2

Why You Should Have a Will

How much are you worth today?

Don't take time to figure it. Just write down an approximate sum quickly. Ask your wife to put down her estimate on a separate sheet of paper. Then, each of you should add in the approximate proceeds of your life insurance policies and any death benefits deriving from your pension plan.

What you will be getting at, of course, is a rough idea of what you each think your estate will be worth. When you compare figures, you could be in for a shock at the disparity of your estimates.

Even if your guesses are similar, how near the actual mark are they? You and your wife might next try to pin down the figures more precisely. (Don't overlook inheritance expectations either of

you may have.) Write down rounded-off sums for
these categories, then add them up.

Equity in your home .... $ _____
Other real estate .... _____
Cash: savings, checking
  accounts; other .... _____
Securities .... _____
Personal property (car, jewelry,
  etc.) .... _____
Face value of personal life
  insurance .... _____
Company life insurance proceeds _____
Pension plan death benefits .... _____
Other assets .... _____
        Total assets at death .... $ _____

At this point, get out records for more accuracy.
What did you overlook or grossly miscalculate?
Take note of those areas which are unclear. That
will help pinpoint what you will need to discuss in
detail later on.

When you write down final figures, be sure you
include the value of jointly-owned property—real
estate, bank accounts, car, whatever. Contrary to
what many persons think, most jointly held property is considered part of the estate of the owner
who dies first. As will be discussed in a later chapter, joint ownership may offer conveniences but is
rarely the way to escape tax bites out of your estate.
And more taxes mean less assets left for your
family.

If you are like most people, you will be surprised
at the actual size of your estate. With today's group
life insurance, rising property values, and compul-
sive habits of amassing "things," couples of even
moderate means often build up estates worth well
over $100,000.

Your estate is everything you possess. In essence, it is also everything that will be distributed in one form or another to other people when you die. A simple concept, perhaps, but not simple in practice. Just look at all the assets most estates include: cash on hand and in the bank; personal articles, such as household goods, art objects, jewelry, stereo equipment, golf clubs; personal life insurance (as opposed to business life insurance); business interests, whether sole ownership, partnership, franchise, or stock in a closed corporation; securities; real estate; miscellaneous items, such as professional accounts receivable, salary due, and so on. The total can be a substantial list to consider.

Without the safeguard of proper planning, your assets may not be received by the people you want to have them. Furthermore, the amount of your estate that is left for distribution after your creditors, administrators, and the tax men take their shares could be a great deal less than what you think you will be leaving behind. **Planning can protect your estate**

That's why careful, knowledgeable estate planning is so important. Laws differ considerably from state to state, and family situations vary greatly. You need an expert to guide you through the intricacies toward the goal you want to achieve. And it is essential that your wife understand how and why these plans have been set up as they have.

Your first step is to show her your will, if you haven't done so already, and discuss it in detail. If you have not yet drawn up a will—or your current will needs updating, as discussed later in this chapter—make plans to do so right away, and involve your wife in the planning.

**The high
cost
of a weak
will**

Your will, when correctly drawn and executed, is a primary instrument for providing that your estate will be distributed according to your wishes, with its value protected from unnecessary shrinkage. Despite its importance, many experts estimate that seven out of eight Americans do not have a proper will. Perhaps because of that so-human tendency to avoid looking at the fact of death, many people have no will at all. This is especially true of women, since our culture tends to associate the need for estate planning not as much with women as with men.

No longer correct

The consequences of a poorly drawn or nonexistent will can be wasteful at best, tragic at worst. In one family, for instance, the husband talked about attending to the making of a will, but he never quite got around to the task. When he died quite suddenly in his early forties, the laws of his state gave only one-third of his estate to his widow, while the other two-thirds went to his nine-year-old daughter. The widow was appointed the child's guardian by the state. This role required her to present detailed reports every year to the court until the girl reached the age of twenty-one, and sometimes that task involved fees for the services of an accountant and an attorney. Moreover, as court-appointed guardian, the mother was required to post a bond of $50,000, which cost over $3,000 in premiums during the next twelve years. Nor could the mother efficiently utilize the child's inheritance. Even procuring money for the girl's education required a formal application to the court . . . and more legal fees.

In another family, a man separated from his wife had gone to live with his sister. By the time of his death he had accumulated a fairly substantial estate. But he made a will on a form he purchased at a stationery store, and the will was declared invalid when he died because several sections did not comply with legal requirements. Thus, he died "intestate"—without a will—and his estate had to be distributed according to the laws of the state in which he lived. When his death was announced, his widow, whom he had not seen for twenty years, rushed to claim her share. She received half the estate by court order. His sister, who had nursed him in sickness and cared for him in health, received only a small settlement, since there were four other brothers and sisters who also shared in the remaining half.

In another case, a retired real estate salesman had painstakingly written a will himself, in his own handwriting. He left most of his modest estate to his sixty-two-year-old wife. But the court would not accept his will as valid, so he, too, died intestate in the eyes of the law. According to the state laws, his widow and each of his five grown children shared equally in the estate—one-sixth for each person. Instead of the financial independence she had expected, the widow had to rely upon her children for support, since her inheritance was insufficient to meet her living expenses. Her children were generous, but she found her dependence humiliating.

Even careful planning can backfire. A well-to-do businessman who left an estate worth about $250,000 had placed most of his property in joint tenancy with his wife to give her sole ownership when he died. Taxes and other costs reduced his estate to about $224,000. When his widow died a few months after her husband, her entire estate—including what she had just inherited—was taxed, too. Although some allowance was made for the fact that taxes had recently been paid on his estate, taxes and settlement costs reduced her estate considerably. If certain trust arrangements had been made in the will, there might have been about $35,000 less to pay in taxes—in other words, about $35,000 more for their children.

All of these situations probably could have been avoided by proper estate planning, which does not begin and end with merely having a will. It involves having the *right kind* of will and the best possible organization of your assets so that your wishes will be carried out.

This chapter discusses facts about wills and how your estate might be handled. Other chapters explore some of the ways you may be able to preserve more of your assets for distribution to your loved ones.

Even if you have a will about which you are reasonably confident, it is essential to discuss these chapters in detail with your wife. She will gain an overall picture of her situation when you are gone and understand why you made certain provisions in certain ways. She also will become familiar with the nature of estate planning, and that knowledge will help her keep her estate plans up to date when she is on her own.

Before you see your lawyer

A will is a plan for the welfare of your wife and children in the event of your death. It indicates that you have given thought to the well-being of your loved ones, and shows unmistakably whom you want to act as executor of your estate, whom you want to assemble and protect the assets you have worked hard to accumulate, whom you want to settle your bills and shoulder the responsibilities you must relinquish.

Before you see your lawyer for the purpose of preparing a will, you should consider carefully all your bequests and other wishes. Do you wish the whole of your estate to go to your wife? Or do you prefer to have some of it held in trust for your children? Do you want your wife to forfeit any of it if she remarries? Who is to be the executor? These are all questions that should be talked over with your wife.

There is the question, too—often overlooked—of how you would want your property handled if you and your wife die together, say, in an automobile accident. This, in turn, leads to the problem of guardianship for minor children and an alternate executor to step in and manage the estate.

A will is a legal instrument, voluntarily made, designed to show how you want everything distributed and managed. If you die without a will—intestate—the state in which you lived will take over the job of dispensing your property. The state operates according to its specific laws, and that may lead to results entirely contrary to your wishes. It also may mean that a much bigger bite comes out of your estate for taxes, administrative fees, and so forth. Remember—when the government and others take more money, your family will receive less. Having a properly drawn will provides the best method of avoiding, or at least minimizing, such a result.

Elements of a will

A will usually has several sections, each with a distinct purpose. There are the "dispositive" clauses, for instance, that parcel out your property and assets to the beneficiaries you designate. And there are "administrative" clauses, which name those persons who are to make sure your instructions are carried out. These persons include the executor, who actually administers the estate, and a guardian, to look after the interests of your minor children.

You also may decide to specify other wishes not so centrally related to the distribution of your assets. Among these could be instructions for paying the expenses of your last illness, plus funeral and burial expenses. (Be sure to make these instructions clear to your wife in another form, since wills are usually read *after* the burial. She should have a copy of your will, and you should write a "last letter of instructions," as outlined in Chapter 11.)

Other special items might involve individual bequests of personal property—your photography equipment to your son, for instance, or your father's watch to your brother. In making such specific bequests, be aware that any minor object mentioned in such a way—even a relatively inexpensive item—may require a special guardian appointed by the court. This could add costs to the handling of your estate. Also, specific bequests can cause complications because the items may have become non-existent or altered by the time of your death.

Your will also may provide for the creation of trusts; cash bequests to charities, loyal secretaries, and any other individual or group you want to mention; and the handling of real estate. Generally, it is wise to describe your legacies as percentages, such as "one-fifth" or "one-half." You thus avoid problems, especially if your estate has shrunk in size since you made your will. For example, say that in your will you bequeathed $10,000 to a specific charity. That dollars-and-cents figure would have to be paid according to your instructions, although the gift might leave little over for your family if your luck had taken a downturn. Specifying a percentage would have been far safer.

These all are possibilities you should talk over with your lawyer and explain to your wife. Very likely, she will have some thoughts to help with your planning.

The executor of your estate will carry out the instructions in your will and wind up your financial affairs, possibly a complicated and time-consuming task. Your wife may not be able to handle such a chore after your death. An executor's duties require that he: **Should your wife be the executor?**

1. Review and arrange for the immediate needs of your survivors.

2. Find proof of your legal residence, marriage, discharge from the armed forces, and other such vital facts.

3. See that all interested parties are notified of your death—your employer, insurance companies, state and federal tax authorities, to name a few.

4. Get waivers from the state tax authorities which will allow your wife to have access to your bank accounts, when appropriate.

5. Assemble evidence of outstanding debts. Examine all such claims and pay the valid ones.

6. Keep records of all transactions and send reports periodically to all concerned.

7. Prepare a full accounting for all beneficiaries and the court.

8. Establish asset values, file necessary tax returns, and obtain necessary death tax clearances.

9. And attend to other duties as needed.

It's no easy job, even for an individual who is as

thoroughly familiar with your financial affairs as your wife should be. Naming a good friend or a relative can have its problems, too. The designated person may have moved far away from your state during the interim. Or he may have died and you may not yet have named a substitute.

Even though a professional executor does charge fees, these are not onerous on most estates. Two and one-half or 3 percent of the total value of the estate is typical in many states, although some states allow higher fees. Having an expert involved could actually save money for your family. Probably your lawyer or banker would be a good choice, in order to provide continuity and expertise. Usually a lawyer belongs to a firm and, should misfortune befall him, his younger associates could take over if necessary. The same goes for your bank: your banker may die but there will be others at the institution to take over. However, in most cases you can name a bank as executor only when the bank has a trust department.

Other executors You might well consider naming a co-executor to share responsibilities with the executor and to take charge if he should die. Your co-executor probably should be someone who you feel will represent your interests in a more personal vein because of closer knowledge of your family and its needs—a brother or sister, a close friend, a child who has reached majority, or your wife. Make sure your wife has a chance to meet and talk with whomever you choose for executor or co-executor. Even if the individual is someone she already knows, it's important that she discuss your will with this person whom you have named.

Also be sure to designate an alternate executor, in case your first choice is unavailable when you die. It's a good idea to state in your will that the alternate may serve without posting a bond. Otherwise, this requirement could be bothersome and costly.

The same care should go into arrangements for any guardian you stipulate to take care of your minor children. This choice is something you and your wife must talk over in detail. Quite naturally, she would be the guardian but, unless you have a proper will, she might have to post a bond until your youngsters are twenty-one years old. Also, don't forget the possibility that you and your wife might die at the same time. Each of you should provide for a guardian other than one another in your respective wills. As you discuss this decision, you might want to talk with your lawyer or banker about the problems and duties of guardianship. For instance, you probably wouldn't want to name your sister, with your brother-in-law as an alternate, when you consider the possibility that your sister may die and your brother-in-law may not know your children well. In such a case, your wife might prefer a member of her family to take over instead.

In discussing the provisions of your will with your wife, you should both realize the importance of her having a will, too. Even if she now has no assets of her own, she will have some after inheriting yours. Her death intestate could cause needless problems and unfair results.

Why your wife should have a will, too

For example, a young woman married a widower with three small children. He drew up a will leaving everything to his new wife, since he knew she would care for his children if he died. But both adults were killed in a car accident, although the wife outlived the husband by a few hours. She had made no will, so the court was obliged by law to give the entire estate to her two brothers. Her husband's three youngsters were left without a dime.

And another example: A wealthy businessman made a bona fide gift of most of his property to his wife in order to reduce taxes on his estate. But she preceded him in death and died intestate. She was without immediate blood relatives, so her estate passed to a cousin with whom she had not had contact in years. The husband received a mere $10,000 of the extensive property he had signed over to his wife.

These may be extreme examples of what goes wrong when a wife leaves no will, but don't make the mistake of thinking, "It couldn't happen to us." It is imperative to involve your wife in your estate planning, so that she will know what to expect when you die, while gaining knowledge about what to include in her own will.

Following are some points you and your wife should consider about your respective wills.

What a will does not cover

There are some assets that cannot be disposed of by will:

1. *Jointly-owned property,* owned by two persons with the right of survivorship, will pass by law to the surviving owner, no matter what provision may be made in the deceased's will. The survivor becomes sole owner.

2. *Insurance policies,* unless made payable to your estate, cannot be affected by your will. If you want to change your beneficiary, you must make the

change on your policy. What you say in your will
has no effect.

3. *U.S. savings bonds,* usually made out in the
name of one person, payable on death to another,
cannot be changed by terms of a will. They must
pass to the person named on the bonds. If no one is
named, they become an asset of your estate.

4. *Death benefits* under company pension plans
will be paid in accordance with the beneficiary des-
ignation you filed with your company.

5. There also are some strange exceptions specified in various state laws. You might find, among
other things, that you may not dispose by will of the
family Bible, farm animals and enough food to care
for them for sixty days, or the family automobile.

In most states, neither spouse may disinherit the
other. Should you draw a will leaving nothing to
your wife, she may invoke a "right of election"
(and so may you if your wife has cut you out of her
will). This permits the surviving spouse to accept
either the provisions of the will or a stated minimum share of the estate, usually the share that
would have been inherited if there had been no will.
In most states this would mean that your wife could
collect at least one-third of your estate.

In the so-called community property states—
Arizona, California, Idaho, Louisiana, Nevada,
New Mexico, Texas, and Washington—it could
mean she would be entitled to one-half.

*LEGAL SOLUTION:
Leave $1 to avoid
this*

Estate planning is complex, whatever the size of
your estate. To ensure that your plans are carried
out, you need a lawyer to state your wishes in the
proper legal language, and to advise you about setting up your affairs in the best way possible. Other-

**How
your lawyer
can help**

wise, it could take years for your estate to go through "probate"—the court procedure that determines if your will is valid and in order—as well as the process of carrying out the instructions you leave in your will.

A will you make yourself can be legal, but it is vulnerable to many mistakes. Even if you draw it up correctly, your lack of knowledge can cause unclear instructions, tax problems, and unnecessary expense. For example, when you refer to "children," does this include your adoptive children? Or, say you leave 200 shares of stock of XYZ Company to your daughter. If that stock splits before your death, you will own 400 shares, and there could be a question at the time of your death about whether your daughter gets 200 or 400 shares. And what about witnesses? Will your secretary suffice? (Not if she is likely to get married and move away.)

Knowing the right answers to questions like these—and acting accordingly—can make all the difference. Unclear provisions may delay settlement of your estate for a long time. Until your estate is settled, your family's inheritance will be held up; there could be problems about what they will live on in the meantime.

So, it's essential to plan carefully and use the services of an expert to help translate your plans into the correct legal instruments. A simple will costs about $50 to prepare. Complex wills can run all the way up to $1,000 or more.

You and your lawyer

Before your first meeting with your lawyer, make a list of your assets and think carefully about what you want to leave your heirs. Also write down the names and addresses of the people you would like to name as executors, guardians, and alternates. (Be sure to confer with them first, and get their permission. That may save complicated changes later on.)

Regard your lawyer as a friend. Tell him everything about your life, your home, your finances, the success or failure of your marriage, your chances for business or professional success in the future. Lawyers aren't called "counselors" through a misuse of terms. That's their principal role—to counsel, to advise, to help. You can consider your lawyer a paid professional friend who is bound by the ethics and standards of his calling to protect your confidences and to act in your best interests.

He will tell you what points should be covered in your will, and he will respect your wishes so far as possible in drawing it up. His main job will be to make certain that it is a binding document and has no legal loopholes or tax problems that can knock your plans awry after you have died.

Your lawyer also will help you and your wife plan your estate in concert with one another. Such joint estate planning is wise, in the sense that a married couple should discuss all matters together and with their lawyer in detail. But don't make the mistake of asking for a joint, husband-and-wife will. Your wife's will should be a wholly separate instrument from yours. A joint will may bring you bargain rates, but you won't simplify matters that way. If anything, a joint will can create ambiguities that will delay settlement of either estate.

Once your will has been drawn, your lawyer will show it to you, probably page by page. If there are any corrections or additions, the entire document

Witnessing your will

may have to be retyped. Not until it is in completed
form, ready to be signed, will he fill in the date.
When the entire document has your approval and
you have indicated your desire to execute it—that
is, to legalize it formally—he will call in witnesses.
The principal restriction in regard to witnesses is
that they may not be named in the will as beneficiaries. All states require at least two witnesses;
some states require three. It is a good idea to have
as witnesses persons who can be located easily.
Your lawyer and members of his staff may be the
easiest—provided, of course, your lawyer's office
routinely keeps track of its secretaries after they
leave their current employment.

Then, before the signing by witnesses, may come
what lawyers call "the little drama," a procedure
that many lawyers are phasing out. In "the little
drama," your lawyer will ask you: "Is this your last
will and testament? Do you wish to make any
changes? Are you satisfied that, as now drawn, it
expresses your will? Are you prepared to execute
this will?"

Then he will ask you to request the witnesses to
witness your signature. You sign your name at the
end of the will, and initial each page. The witnesses
make it official by signing their names and
addresses.

As a final precaution, the lawyer will fasten the
pages of the will together in such a way that they
cannot be removed, or even opened, without showing
that they have been tampered with. This involves a
stapling machine, ribbon, or sealing wax, and sometimes all three. Then the will is inserted into an envelope and sealed, and you are asked to write your
signature across the envelope and flap (again, so
that if there is any premature tampering with the

envelope, it would be immediately evident).

The procedure may seem a bit melodramatic and, indeed, many lawyers are no longer quite so formal. However, "the little drama" points out the seriousness of the matter at hand and the importance of the proper legalities. The legal force attached to a will is immense. For example, in the event you sign more than one copy of your will, all signed copies must be produced before the will can be probated; otherwise, there is the presumption that you may have wanted the will revoked.

Among the hazards of drawing up a will without legal counsel is the requirement that the language be exact, according to law. Under federal law, for instance, your wife is entitled to a marital deduction that effectively reduces the taxes on your estate. However, she may not qualify if you fail to use the proper terminology in your will. Once again, the importance of a lawyer is evident.

The dangers of do-it-yourself wills

In addition to the variety of will that is drafted by a lawyer, there are two other forms. One is to be avoided, the other used only in case of emergency. The first is the "holographic" will, written entirely in the handwriting of the testator (the person who is doing the bequeathing). This type of will requires no witnesses, but it is more frequently rejected than probated. A majority of states do not consider such a will valid. If you have such a will, it is advisable to take it to your lawyer and let him use it as a basis for drawing up a proper will. Only a limited number of states and territories permit holographic wills.

The second kind of will is the "nuncupative," or oral, will. Most states will recognize these only if

made by a soldier or sailor while in military service
or by a mariner while at sea. There need not be immediate peril of death in order for the will to be
uttered. At least two witnesses are necessary—
neither of them beneficiaries, of course. And there
are rigid time limits on the validity of such a will.

**Changing
your
will**
Despite the widespread belief to the contrary, a
will *can* be revoked, changed, or destroyed by its
author. This flexibility is one of the advantages of
a will: it does not become effective until you die.

You may revoke your will by a written statement.
This is a highly technical procedure, however, and
should be done only with a lawyer's assistance. A
formal revocation is just as painstakingly executed
as the will itself. Even a notarized statement of revocation cannot be accepted in many probate courts.

If you destroy your will, you may incur the possibility that your survivors and former beneficiaries
will try to prove in court that you did not destroy
the will with *intent to revoke,* and they may suc-
ceed in having the terms of the will invoked by
court decree. So the best way to revoke a will is to
let your lawyer do it. He will make the original null
and void by executing a new will stating that it
revokes all prior wills, and by physically destroying
the old will.

If you want only to change your will—because
there has been an addition to your estate, for instance—you can make an addition, or supplement,
to your present will in the form of a *codicil.* When
you revoke a will, you must revoke all codicils, too.

Be sure you and your wife keep your wills up to
date. Family fortunes change, sometimes subtly,
and those changes often can bring about the need

to alter estate plans. Any number of circumstances can necessitate such updating. Both you and your wife should go over the following checklist now; if you answer any of the questions affirmatively, consider changing your wills accordingly. If there is no need for present change, keep the questions in mind as a constant alert for future updating of estate plans.

When to consider changing your will

Any new members in the family? Baby? *(check off)* Adoptions? One of your children married? Grandchild? _____

Any change in your status? New marriage? Separation? Divorce? _____

Have you moved to another state? _____

Has your lawyer or executor moved to another state? _____

Have the inheritance laws in your state changed? _____

Has a witness, executor, guardian, or trustee died? _____

Has your estate grown considerably? Did you buy or inherit significant additional property or assets? _____

Have you sold your house or bought a new one? _____

How about the status of your beneficiaries? Have any died, married, or divorced? _____

Have the needs of any of your beneficiaries changed? _____

Do you want to change beneficiaries? _____

Does setting up a trust fund seem like a good idea? _____

Have you made any major gifts or loans? _____

Safeguarding your will

It is *not* a good idea to keep the signed original of your will in your safe deposit box, contrary to what might be supposed to be the proper residing place for such an important document. The reason: the bank usually must seal the box—even if it is co-owned by you and your wife—until an opening is cleared by the tax authorities. There are some exceptions, but you should count on a delay of several days. Problems also could arise if the key to the box is lost. Keep a copy of the will in the box, if you like, and another at home. But give the signed original to your lawyer or banker for safekeeping and ready access. They have special vaults for such purposes.

Above all, don't move your will about frequently or with secrecy. Let your wife and lawyer know where it is, and be sure you know where your wife's will is kept. You have a will drawn for one purpose only, to apportion your property after death to those whom you want to benefit from it; so don't make finding your will a hazardous game of hide-and-seek. If it is not located, your good intentions may be wasted. One of the classic tales of careless storage, it may be recalled, relates to the will disposing of Hetty Green's $90-million estate. It was discovered by accident under a soap dish in her house.

Wherever your will is kept, attach a note stating in bold letters: "Caution: Do Not Open. This Is an Original Will; Any Alteration or Tampering May Void the Will." Be sure your wife observes the same rule.

CHAPTER 3

Your House:
Keep It
or
Sell It?

We're all familiar with the classic scene from the melodrama: a poor widow, her children clustered at her knees, driven from her home into the blinding snow because she cannot pay the mortgage. It seems a gross exaggeration when played on the stage—but it is not an impossibility in real life! Not that mortgage bankers have long, black mustaches and hearts of ice. On the contrary, their business codes are designed to see that the chances of a client's losing a homestead is minimized. The law provides some safeguards, too.

Still, careless planning can make things difficult for your widow. So why not provide for her peace of mind? It is easy these days to see that your mortgage will be paid off automatically if you die. And

it is not much more difficult to see that there will be
enough regular income to pay a reasonable rent
each month indefinitely, if that is your wife's preference.

To cover your mortgage, most lenders offer what
is called *decreasing term* insurance at a nominal
fee. The cost often is worked right into your
monthly payments, averaged out to cover the entire
period. With this kind of policy, the amount of insurance lessens as the amount you owe shrinks,
until the mortgage is completely paid off. If you die
before the mortgage ends, the balance is paid immediately. Your widow has no more payments to
make; she owns the house outright. A typical policy
of this sort, bought at age thirty, on a $35,000,
thirty-year mortgage, would cost about $170 a year.

This probably is the cheapest insurance you can
buy for the task; the rate is low because the policy
builds up no cash value—in other words, has no
built-in savings program. Some banks can offer it
as group insurance, spreading the risk (and therefore the cost) over the averages of a great number
of borrowers. In that case, about $135 would be
added to your mortgage payments each year to
cover the insurance.

Another choice is to buy "ordinary" or "whole"
life insurance that builds up cash value while it
gives you full protection. You even could figure it
so that when the cash value equals the amount of
mortgage you have outstanding—exactly when
depends upon complicated mathematics—you can
simply cash in the policy and pay off the rest of the
mortgage.

There are many ways to make the most of life
insurance, as the next chapter shows in more detail.
In terms of your wife's living situation, one possi-

bility is to use insurance to ensure that she will have regular income for rent money. A $50,000 ordinary life policy on your life bought at age thirty-five, for instance, would give her a nest egg that could pay over $200 a month when invested at, say, 5 percent per year, compounded quarterly, and the principal would not be depleted at all. You might leave the policy proceeds to her outright, with the understanding that she would put it in some productive and safe place, such as in a savings bank. Or you could save on estate taxes by creating a trust for the entire amount, with the income going to her throughout her life, and the principal going to your children when she dies. There also are possibilities of insurance annuity contracts, as well as other arrangements.

Whatever your provisions, it is essential that the two of you discuss in detail how your wife would like to live after she is widowed. Small children pose one set of problems. Grown children bring other considerations. Many variables must be thought about, depending upon your situation.

What you both must measure is the degree to which the home lies at the heart of her sense of security, and to what extent it reflects—or can reflect—her general tastes and life style. That goes for apartments as well as houses, and the implications should be talked over thoughtfully. A couple in Maryland, for instance, had lived for years in a country home that had belonged to his family. They enjoyed a comfortable, outdoor way of life in that rambling old house while their three children grew up. But then the husband died, just as the youngest child was finishing college. The wife was left with

Your wife's feelings about her home

a house much too large for her needs, little cash to pay for household help, and sky-high property taxes in what had become a rapidly developing neighborhood.

The clear decision would have been to sell the house, but she was reluctant to do so. She had been happy there. And she felt it had been important to her husband to retain the family homestead. They had never discussed the matter, however; the house was just something they took for granted as an essential part of their life. Yet, now she was faced with an agonizing decision. It could have been handled much more easily if she and her husband had clarified the choices together in advance. Eventually, she had to sell anyway, but only after she had spent considerable money trying to hold and maintain the house.

Among questions of general life style which a husband and wife should discuss are these: How important is it that your children and your wife remain in the same familiar neighborhood? Can your wife manage the house on her own? Will her pride get in the way of practicality? Are you perhaps underestimating her abilities? On the other hand, will she need a place quite so large? Will the house provide a feeling of social and financial security? Or will it cause anxiety without you around? Has she secretly thought of living in some other location? Would a move make her life easier by bringing her closer to stores and other conveniences?

Such questions are difficult, especially since they may touch upon previously unspoken thoughts and feelings. It is important for you both to be patient and understanding—and honest. To help, remember that this can be *life* planning, too. Your conversations could well lead to fresh insight and positive action that will improve your marriage and family life immediately. You will also help pave the way to the right mutual decisions about how and where you want to live when you retire.

If you are like most families, your house is the largest investment in your life. Your widow probably will not be in any emotional condition at the time of your death to make a quick decision about your home. Nor should she do so. Even though you two talk about the possibilities now, she should take time after you die to figure out, among other things, exactly how much it costs her to stay where she is and how that compares with the alternatives. She should understand how real estate is valued, how she can use real property to her advantage, where the significant costs lie and what they are, what unforeseen expenses and other problems might arise.

The dollars-and-cents value of home owning

How much is your house worth right now, for instance? How much is it likely to be worth a few years from now? There are a number of ways to find out. For the most accurate present figure, you can call in a professional appraiser. He will charge from about $75 to $200 to examine everything from the building itself to the market value in terms of your neighborhood, proximity to services, general prices, and so forth. Actually, you can gain a fairly good idea on your own by scouting prices of houses similar to yours in the immediate vicinity. If you have a friend who is a realtor, he may give you an informal professional estimate. Another approach is to ask your local banker how much you could borrow against your house right now.

Whatever your means of investigation, one thing is almost certain: Your house is worth considerably more today than it was when you bought it. That is the important lesson for your wife to learn. In these days of rising costs with no real relief from inflation in sight, your home can be not only your largest asset, but also the one most likely to keep ahead of the inflation game. Between mid-1968 and mid-1974, the average selling price of a "used" house rose dramatically throughout the country, according to the Federal Home Loan Bank Board. Typical figures: up 90 percent in Atlanta, 48 percent in Boston, 50 percent in Denver, 67 percent in Minneapolis-Saint Paul, 48 percent in the Los Angeles-Long Beach area.

During those same six years, Federal Housing Administration (FHA) figures show that the average purchase prices of new houses rose 28 percent, from $19,400 to $26,864. The average size of houses grew during that period, which may account for some of the rise in price. But average building lots became smaller at the same time, so one can figure that the bulk of appreciation in value was real. There can be no question that houses cost more each day. Land prices for federally insured homes have increased at an average annual rate of about 13 percent since 1968, for instance, and costs for labor and materials have risen almost as fast.

Accelerated values can benefit the current homeowner who may sell later on. But they can be detrimental to the potential home buyer: he will have to invest more money a few years from now than he would at present for the same size of used or new house. These are facts that your wife may have to weigh on her own some day.

She also should understand that a house provides

borrowing leverage. There are second mortgages, for instance—once considered by many people to be an embarrassment, but now used increasingly. More and more lenders are offering second mortgages, and it is possible to get a good sum of money —typically, several thousand dollars—through such loans. The rates are not as low as those on a first mortgage, and the time period is shorter. (Specific terms are dictated by state law.) Also, people on fixed incomes—such as widows—may have a more difficult time getting second mortgages. Still, second mortgages are worth knowing about, since your wife could probably borrow more money this way than with regular loans, and interest rates are competitive with such loans. Perhaps more important, it is not necessary to refinance the present mortgage to get the needed cash. Thus, she would retain the original loan, which probably has a lower rate than she could find on a new loan. And, it is possible there will be fewer closing costs associated with a second mortgage than when refinancing an old mortgage.

What's more, most lenders do not impose restrictions on the use of that money. It might be used for home improvement, to buy a vacation home or boat, or to help pay for college. That last possibility is especially important for the young widow to realize. True, she would be incurring an extra debt that would have to be paid off monthly for several years. But if your children are college age, it is quite possible your widow could be working, so there would be extra income to handle such a debt. However, she should consult her lawyer and a financial adviser before entering into this type of agreement.

Uses of a second mortgage

Second mortgages are usually figured in terms of the equity you have in your house. ("Equity" is the portion of your house you actually own—in other words, the part you have paid off. Your down payment is the foundation of equity when you buy a house, and each month the equity grows by the amount of your payment that goes toward principal rather than interest.) Many bankers will allow you to borrow up to 70 or 80 percent or even more of your equity. That means if you had a $15,000 equity in your house from a $25,000 twenty-year mortgage (you would have that after about fifteen years), you could borrow about $9,000 or more on a second mortgage, at rates comparable to those of regular consumer loans.

If your widow did not have much equity built up yet, she might consider refinancing the mortgage to get extra cash. However, caution her that such a step can pose problems. For one thing, she might have to take out the new mortgage at a higher interest rate. For another, unless she refinances with the same lender, there could be penalties when she pays off the old loan with money from the new one. And there might be several hundred dollars in new costs for title search and insurance, appraisals, and so forth. She will need good legal and financial counsel in this instance. Whatever the course of action, the house does give your wife a financial leverage she otherwise might not have.

What is a mortgage? A widow taking on a new mortgage, refinancing an old one, or buying a second mortgage should understand how mortgages work. A mortgage is a debt incurred for the purchase of property. It has two parts: the "note," which is the IOU that states the terms under which repayment is promised; and the "mortgage," or "deed of trust," with which you pledge the property as security to the lender, so he can take it over if you fail to meet your mortgage payments.

A number of variables are possible with mortgages, and it takes some knowledge and smart shopping to get what you want. These contingencies can make your wife's life easier or more difficult when she takes over the house and must continue to pay off the mortgage, or when she decides to sell. Knowing about these variations also will help her if she buys a house on her own. Among things to look for and evaluate:

Are there *prepayment penalties,* so that it would cost you extra money if you paid off part or all of the mortgage earlier? Loans insured by the Veterans Administration (VA) have none, although they require that the advance payments be made in specific sums. FHA and conventional mortgages have varying requirements.

Is there a *"balloon clause,"* which makes monthly payments less, but requires that the remainder of the loan be paid off at a stipulated time in a lump sum? This provision is something to be wary of, especially if you are taking over a previous owner's mortgage. If you are not prepared to meet the lump-sum payment when it is due, you might have to refinance at a higher interest rate.

Must you maintain an *escrow account* with the lender? This would increase your monthly payment in order to provide a fund for paying your property taxes and insurance each year. It can be a good means of money management, but you might prefer to handle such matters on your own.

What about *assumption rights?* Usually a lender

will write some clause into your mortgage reserving his right to pass judgment on any potential buyer for your house, since that new buyer might be assuming your mortgage. With such latitude the lender could possibly turn down a buyer unless, say, the interest rate were raised—which would make your house a less attractive buy. When you purchase initially, see if your lawyer can include a clause in your mortgage preventing the lender from unreasonably withholding approval of an otherwise qualified buyer. Also try to have the purchase contract state that the buyer is assuming the mortgage at the current rate. The terms should be spelled out very clearly, because the new note takes precedence over whatever the old note may have said. Finally, watch out for an assumption clause that would make you personally, liable if the buyer defaults.

There also are a number of *settlement costs*— often referred to as "closing costs"—that may be negotiable to some extent, and could add several hundred dollars to your expenses otherwise, usually at the time you sign the mortgage contract. Many of these costs are handled in specific ways, depending upon local practice within various communities, and there may not be much you can negotiate. However, it's always worth a try. Here are some settlement costs to discuss with your wife:

1. *Title insurance.* Your lender probably will require you to buy it to cover him against the possibility that there is a hidden claim to ownership of part or all of your property. Be sure you also get "owner's" title insurance, to cover you for the same thing. The additional cost is negligible.

2. *Insurance on your life*, to pay off the mortgage if you die.

3. *Property insurance.* Your lender will insist upon being named as an insured party in your home owner's policy, to cover his investment. These policies vary widely, and you should get an expert's advice before buying. (See the end of this chapter.)

4. *Insurance against default.* Mortgages insured by the FHA and the VA are primarily concerned with default. The government is insuring your lender against the possibility that you may not meet your payments. Some private companies have joined the government in selling this kind of mortgage insurance, and the costs will be included in the loan. Such insurance encourages a lender to assume more risks—usually in the form of a lower down payment, which leaves more to pay back—and you should realize that *you* will be footing the bill ultimately.

5. *Points.* These are extra costs the lender charges for services such as legal work, credit checks, appraisal costs, and so forth. You may pay these altogether when you sign the contract, or they may be spread out in your monthly payments. In many cases, you thus will be paying interest on such service charges.

How mortgage interest works

Unlike installment loans, where interest is figured on the original balance, mortgage interest is figured on the current principal balance each month. Early in the loan you pay more in interest and less in principal, and eventually it is the other way around. Toward the end of the loan period, you pay very little in interest each month, and the principal payments snowball. With that, your equity builds dramatically.

Explain the arithmetic to your wife. Say you

borrow $25,000 at 7½ percent annual interest for thirty years. Your monthly payments for principal and interest are $174.81. The first payment covers interest calculated on the entire $25,000 loan and $18.56 of principal. (Figure interest by one-twelfth —for twelve months in the year—of 7½ percent of $25,000. That's $1,875 divided by twelve, to get $156.25. Then subtract $156.25 from $174.81 to get $18.56.) The next month the principal of the loan has been reduced to $24,981.44 ($25,000 minus $18.56), and the interest falls to $156.13 a month; your principal that month increases to $18.68. And so it goes. By year's end you will own approximately $235 more of the house, and all the rest of your payments that year (approximately $1,863) will be tax-deductible as interest on a loan.

Because of this method of calculating interest, you will pay off less than 1 percent of the principal in the first year of the loan and about 6 percent at the end. The example in the following table of a thirty-year, $25,000 mortgage at 7½ percent shows how much principal remains to be paid at various time periods. (The percentages will differ slightly when the interest is at a different rate. Banks have detailed tables showing the variations.)

Equity growth rate in relation to time of mortgage

($25,000, thirty-year mortgage at 7½ percent interest)

Length of time payments have been made	*Percentage of principal you still must pay off*
5 years	94.6%
10 years	88.6%
15 years	78.0%
20 years	62.7%
25 years	40.4%

There are several significant implications in this table. For one thing, if you sell your house early into the mortgage, much of the purchase price you receive must be used to pay off the principal still owed. Unless your house has appreciated considerably in value during that short period of time, you won't be making much money; in fact, most of your money has gone toward interest.

For another thing, the more principal you pay off early in the loan, the more interest you will save and the less the loan will cost you overall. That is because interest is figured on the outstanding principal balance of the loan. The earlier you pay off principal the better (provided you do not trigger any prepayment penalties). For instance, if you had a $25,000 loan at 7½ percent for thirty years, the monthly payment for principal and interest would be $174.81. In the ninth month of that loan, only $19.51 of the payment reduces the principal, and $155.30 goes for interest. Now, if in the preceding month you had paid $174.81 *plus* $19.51 (the principal for the following month), you would shorten the loan period by a month. If you kept on prepaying that way (or in any amount allowed by your loan), you would hasten final payment, and ultimately save considerable interest.

Such fancy mathematics may not be the prime concern for a widow, especially if she is an older woman who may be less worried about questions of equity and long-term savings. But your wife should be aware that she may face special problems if she wants to buy a different house after you have died.

There are times when it is difficult to obtain financing, for instance. In that case, your wife might have better luck if she can offer a large down payment—assuming she does not need all the cash for something else, such as college tuition for your children. The bulk of the down payment may come from money you have left her, or from profit when she sells the current house.

Aside from getting financing more readily with a large down payment, she will have less to pay out each month. This table shows why:

To buy a $30,000 house
(Mortgage figured for twenty years at 7½ percent interest per year)

Down payment		Mortgage amount	Monthly payment
Percentage of purchase price	*Dollar amount*		
10%	$3,000	$27,000	$199.60
25%	$7,500	$22,500	$166.30
40%	$12,000	$18,000	$133.10

With a larger down payment, not only will her monthly payments be less, but she will have a greater equity in the house to begin with. And that means that if she were to die, her heirs would be getting more house and less debt. One must always remember, however, that making a larger down payment removes cash that perhaps should better be kept on hand for other major expenses.

Property taxes   Along with recognizing the benefits of owning a home, your wife should understand its drawbacks, too. Maintenance costs and other expenses, such as heating, can be considerable. Also, although the home owner can take mortgage interest and property taxes as income tax deductions each year, how

Elderly Carry Heavy Burden of Real Estate Taxes

In some areas of the Northeast, where taxes are high, property levies take almost $30 out of each $100 of incomes of the elderly poor.

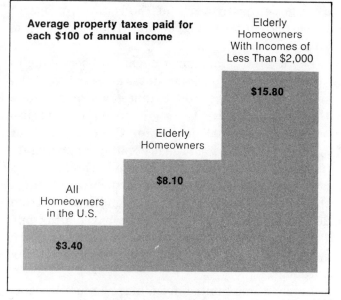

Average property taxes paid for each $100 of annual income

Elderly Homeowners With Incomes of Less Than $2,000

$15.80

Elderly Homeowners

$8.10

All Homeowners in the U.S.

$3.40

Source: Advisory Commission on Intergovernmental Relations

much real advantage does this offer a widow in a low income tax bracket?

Property taxes in particular are a constant concern. Until action is taken to bring these taxes down, many home owners will continue to find the levies extremely burdensome. In 1972, according to the U.S. Advisory Commission on Intergovernmental Relations, the average property taxes paid by all home owners for each $100 of annual income was $3.40. But for elderly home owners, it was $8.10, and for those with incomes of less than $2,000, the average was $15.80. In other words, a widow who owned her home and received $6,000 income might have to pay $486 in property taxes—almost one month's income! Even a widow with a $10,000 income might find her bill almost 8 percent of her annual income. And that's only the national average; in many parts of the country, property taxes take an even bigger bite. They tend to rise steadily, too.

Fortunately, state governments are beginning to attack this problem. Some states already have "circuit breaker" laws, for instance, which stipulate that when property taxes go above a certain proportion of personal income for the elderly, all or some of the excess charge is credited against state income tax or is paid out in cash to the home owner. Even renters may benefit from such laws, where the assumption is made that the landlord uses from 20 to 25 percent of their rent to pay his tax bill. Other states use federal funds, such as those from revenue sharing, to help relieve the property tax burden.

Persons on a limited, fixed income must be especially concerned about property taxes. If your wife plans to move after your death, she should explore the tax situation carefully wherever she looks. She should be aware that property taxes may rise considerably in neighborhoods where there are many young people and the need for schools will burgeon.

What housing choices are there? Although widows face some problems in common, individual situations differ considerably. Think of all the questions of size, convenience, cost, and methods of ownership, sale, or rental that bear upon the decision of whether or not to sell the home:

If a widow wants to sell, for instance, should she use the services of a real estate agent? She will pay about 6 or 7 percent of the selling price as his fee. But his knowledge and energy may net her

more for the house even so. (Whatever the ultimate decision, it might be a good idea for the two
of you to discuss the matter in general terms with
a real estate agent now. Even if you make it clear to
him—and you should do so—that the discussion
does not automatically assure him the business now
or later, he is likely to be helpful. Public relations
are important to him, and he knows that he could
be paving the way for business in the future.)

Should your wife hang on to the house and rent
out part of it to bring in extra money? One hundred
or more dollars in rent could be important monthly
income, but she had better be fairly sure she will
like having a boarder around before she makes that
decision.

Should she sell the house and rent an apartment?
Various figures have been marshalled to demon-
state that renting is cheaper than home owning,
despite the tax and equity advantages of having
your own house. On the other hand, an equal vol-
ume of statistics prove the case the other way
around. The question of apartment rental often
gets down to life-style preference. Will your wife
want to live in a building with many other people?
How important are the maintenance and security
conveniences of apartment living? How much living space does she need? (Don't overlook provisions for visiting offspring and grandchildren.)

One possibility: She can buy an apartment in a
cooperative or condominium. These arrangements
provide some of the tax and equity advantages of
home ownership, without the maintenance head-
aches. With a *cooperative,* she purchases shares in
a corporation which owns the apartment building,
grounds, and all facilities. Her shares give her a
certain percentage of ownership of the entire com-

plex but she does not own her apartment. With a *condominium,* she does own an apartment, plus a certain percentage of the common property as well.

Either arrangement allows a specified amount of her monthly "maintenance charges" to be taken as a tax deduction. That percentage is considered to be the portion of her payment that has gone toward property taxes and mortgage interest for the entire property or building. Some people prefer condominiums to co-ops because one can buy and sell a condominium apartment as a piece of real estate, which may entail mortgage financing rather than the usually higher-priced personal loan financing required in many places for co-ops. Another big advantage a condominium has over a cooperative is that the owner of a condominium has absolute ownership of his apartment without regard to whether or not the other owners pay their shares. In a co-op, the entire building can be foreclosed by a mortgage holder or other creditor even if you have made all your proper payments.

Remember, if your wife does not pay cash for her co-op or condominium (as well she may, from her inheritance), she will have to pay off the mortgage financing each month in addition to her regular maintenance charges. On the other hand, financing for co-ops and condominiums may be easier for single women (including widows) to secure than is money for a house. Apparently, many lenders think women can better maintain an apartment than a house, and conclude that the property—and therefore the investment—will hold up better.

Condominiums especially are coming into vogue. Look at all the well-advertised retirement or second-home communities which offer this arrangement along with houses ideal for one or two people.

Many legitimate developers are in this business, and you can find very satisfactory arrangements. But there are many unscrupulous developers, too. Unfortunately, the latter often use sales techniques simulating those employed by honest businessmen. If your wife thinks she might like to move to one of these communities, she should investigate the developer first, through the Interstate Land Sales Office, in Washington, D.C., as well as her local Better Business Bureau, banker, and other persons or institutions she can trust.

Widows are prime targets for fraud. They often have just inherited large sums of money, and they are presumed to be uninformed about money matters. Your wife should *never* sign a piece of paper for any property deal without consulting her lawyer first.

If she finds she has committed herself inadvertently on paper, the law provides certain protections, and she may have a three-day "cooling off" period, during which she can repudiate the contract. Even so, there are many ways she could sign away her rights unwittingly. Emphasize to her the importance of using expert counsel in any arrangement involving much money.

Do not forget to give yourself the same advice. The government estimates that tens of millions of dollars are lost every year by victims of land sales frauds. The losers are not all widows. Many are couples planning for retirement, or individuals looking for a quick way to make a dollar. Anyone is vulnerable to these schemes. What you might lose through carelessness or naiveté now is money lost for your future life together, or for your widow's protection during the years following your death.

What to look for in a new home

Suppose your wife decides to move to an apartment or a different house. In addition to questions of size and cost, there are many factors to consider. A home is not just a roof over her head, after all. A home includes a neighborhood, a school district, friends for your children and wife, financial security (or stress), an entire way of life.

You both should look over the following checklist to be reminded of some of the considerations involved when deciding where to live. Many of the questions apply to apartment dwellers as well as home owners. Some are important if you are young, some more pertinent if you are older. Some bear on the ages of your children and whether they still live with you. Furthermore, most of these questions are not solely for a widow to consider. They apply equally well whether as a couple you are contemplating moving soon, or whether you are thinking ahead to retirement:

● *What is the "feel" of the neighborhood as you drive around?*

Are yards and homes well kept?

Are there street potholes and plugged-up storm sewers?

Many children playing outdoors? (Youngsters usually reflect families with stability and strong community interest, since families are likely to remain settled until the school years end. Families also can suggest rising property taxes.)

Are the streets well lighted at night?

How about shopping areas?

What are the people like? Do they seem friendly in the supermarkets? Cordial when you ask questions? Involved with other people?

● *What about zoning?*

Are big houses divided into apartments or rooming houses? (Disintegrating exteriors and a number of cars in the driveway can be signs.) Such a breakdown in housing often betrays a declining neighborhood, or one with a high rate of transiency.

Would zoning restrictions interfere with activities you plan to engage in, such as making furniture for sale in your basement, or building with prefabricated materials? Check the town clerk's office.

Are new highways planned? Where will heavy traffic be routed?

What about factories? Trucking routes?

Are the zoning laws actually enforced? (You can get an idea by looking at old issues of the local paper, where there may be stories of zoning battles, changes, variances, and a reflection of the local point of view.)

● *How good are the schools?*

What are average class sizes?

Are medical personnel on the staff?

How much money is allotted to each pupil in the school budget?

Is the Parent-Teacher Association active?

How modern and commodious are the school facilities?

● *What about other services?*

You can check out the fire department in a large city with the American Insurance Association and with the state insurance-rating bureau in smaller communities. As for police departments, the local rates for theft insurance will tell a tale.

What is the ratio of policemen to people? What do individuals in the community say about the quality of their protection?

Is garbage collection free? Adequate?

Are there easily accessible libraries, museums,

public parks, a swimming pool, and other recreational facilities?

Are there local activities such as Boy Scout and Girl Scout troops?

What about hospitals? Clinics? Public transportation? Churches? Theaters? How far away?

● *What are the local taxes?*

Find out about *all* of them, as well as special assessments for sewage disposal, street lighting, and any other local improvement likely to increase costs.

Is tax money being put to good use, or are taxes high and services poor?

The importance of home insurance   Wherever your wife chooses to live, she must be covered by insurance which will protect her home and belongings against disasters such as fire or theft. This is called homeowner's insurance (there are special policies for apartment dwellers), and it is important to have expert advice about what type of coverage to buy. The more expensive the policy, the more extensive the coverage, although usually one cannot buy protection at all against some kinds of disaster, such as floods. (There are some tax breaks for victims of such tragedies, however.)

Aside from being certain that she is covered appropriately against all probable dangers, your widow must take care to update her insurance periodically. Most insurers insist a house be insured for at least 80 percent of its replacement value, or they will not cover a partial loss completely. Don't forget, costs of labor and materials are rising rapidly. What would have been a $1,000 replacement a few years ago could cost $1,500 now. If insurance is not kept up to the 80-percent mark, losses may be

Types of Property Insurance

Forms   *Perils*

1. fire or lightning

2. loss of property removed from premises endangered by fire or other perils

3. windstorm or hail

4. explosion

5. riot or civil commotion

6. aircraft

7. vehicles

8. smoke

9. vandalism and malicious mischief

10. theft

11. breakage of glass constituting a part of the building

12. falling objects

13. weight of ice, snow, sleet

14. collapse of building(s) or any part thereof

15. sudden and accidental tearing asunder, cracking, burning, or bulging of a steam or hot water heating system or of appliances for heating water

16. accidental discharge, leakage or overflow of water or steam from within a plumbing, heating or air-conditioning system or domestic appliance

17. freezing of plumbing, heating and air-conditioning systems and domestic appliances

18. sudden and accidental injury from artificially generated currents to electrical appliances, devices, fixtures and wiring (TV and radio tubes not included)

All perils *EXCEPT:* earthquake, landslide, flood, surface water, waves, tidal water or tidal wave, the backing up of sewers, seepage, war, and nuclear radiation.

(Forms bracket labels: Basic, Broad, Comprehensive)

Source: Insurance Information Institute

figured in terms of depreciation, making it necessary to spend a good deal out of pocket to repair
damages.

An Idaho widow lived in the house she and her
husband had owned. Fifteen years after her husband's death, the house had a replacement value of
$40,000. But she had maintained the old homeown-
er's policy at $26,000; premiums were low and she
was unaware of the 80-percent rule. Then a fire destroyed her roof and damaged a room. It cost $5,000
to replace the roof and $1,500 to fix the room. How-
ever, the roof had been installed ten years earlier.
Guaranteed for twenty years, it had depreciated
half its expected lifetime. Since she had not met the
80-percent rule, the insurance paid only half the replacement costs of the roof, or $2,500. They also
deducted for depreciation on the room, so she had
to pay over $3,000 out of her savings to get the re-
pair job done.

This woman was lucky not to have suffered a
more destructive fire. If the house had been destroyed completely, she could have recovered only
the $26,000 face value of her policy. Had she main-
tained 80 percent insurance, she at least would have
recovered $32,000; and 90 percent would have given
her $36,000. (No one can collect more than the sum
total of insurance stipulated.) Considering that she
probably would have lost personal property worth
thousands of dollars in the fire, too, and may have
had to pay off the old mortgage as well as finance a
new one (no doubt at a higher rate), the low insurance she maintained could have been even more dis-
astrous.

Homeowner's insurance also provides a policy
holder with several other kinds of coverage: some
liability insurance in case an individual is hurt on

the premises or—in certain cases—if you or a member of your family cause injury to someone elsewhere; in some circumstances medical payments to an individual who is hurt on your property; damage to property—yours, or someone else's; some living expenses, in case of fire or other severe damage to your house. Most personal property also is covered, usually up to 50 percent of the face value of the overall policy when the property is on the premises. (Depreciation is figured on personal property.) Coverage on specific kinds of items is limited, however; extra insurance is needed for items such as fur coats, jewelry, and works of art.

Most homeowners' policies cover the policy holder "off premises," too. This gives protection for up to 10 percent of the face value of the policy for losses outside the home—when you are robbed on vacation, for instance, or even while taking the bus to work. Off-premises coverage is not available in some places, such as New York City, for example. Expensive items, such as cameras, should be covered separately. Coverage against crime is becoming increasingly difficult to buy, even for a home. In an area where it is not possible to get such protection, you may be able to buy federal crime insurance, or special insurance from the state. Often agents do not tell clients about these policies. A call to the state insurance office, or possibly the business or insurance editor of the local newspaper, should determine whether such insurance is available.

With all these questions to think about, it is especially important that your wife meet and talk with your insurance agent now, and that they agree to keep up a continuing dialogue through the years.

4

Producing an "Instant Estate"

For most families, life insurance holds a key place in their plans for financial security. Experts strongly caution against risking money in any investment until a sound savings plan *and* an adequate insurance program have first been established.

The accepted rule of thumb for *savings* is to keep the equivalent of three months' or more salary available in readily liquid assets, such as a bank account. If your income is irregular—perhaps you earn commissions—the recommendation is to keep an equivalent of at least six months' of your average earnings.

It is less easy to decide how much insurance you need. Various formulas are cited. Some experts say "three to five times your annual salary." Others recommend as much as $200,000 if you are in your mid-thirties and have children—even more if you are younger! The fact is that there are many variables in family circumstances and insurance policies. To arrive at the right insurance program for yourself and your wife requires an intelligent awareness of your needs, your wishes, and the possibilities available to you.

A life insurance policy is a contract whereby a company guarantees to pay your survivor a stipulated sum upon your death in return for regular payments ("premiums") while you are alive. One person may take out a policy and pay only a few dollars before he dies, leaving a sizable sum to his heirs. Another may live to go on paying for years. Insurance companies have figured out life expectancy "actuarially," which means they know that a certain percentage of policyholders will die at a certain age. Overall life expectancy figures determine how much you will pay each year.

Life insurance companies have their figures worked out so that they do not lose money. If some hapless chap takes out a policy for $10,000 and pays $250 for his first year's premiums, then immediately gets killed by a truck, obviously the company that sold him the policy has "lost" money. But at the end of twenty years, or forty or fifty, during which most policyholders live, the companies have earned a substantial amount of money. They have accurately determined the odds on how long how many policyholders do live and thus will pay premiums steadily.

What happens to the premiums you pay? The companies invest the money in stocks, bonds, mortgages, real estate, and other ventures. By and large,

Causes of Death of U.S. Policyholders
1945-1974

Cause of Death	1945	1950	1955	1960	1965	1970	1974
Natural Causes							
Cardiovascular-renal ...	49.3%	57.0%	57.2%	55.7%	53.9%	52.1%	50.4%
Cancer	14.8	17.3	18.6	18.7	19.2	20.1	20.7
Pneumonia and influenza	3.1	1.9	2.0	3.2	3.1	3.3	2.7
Tuberculosis (all forms) .	2.8	1.3	.5	.3	.2	.1	.1
Diabetes	1.5	1.3	.9	1.0	1.1	1.0	1.1
Other diseases*	18.2	12.0	12.3	13.1	13.6	14.5	16.1
Total	89.7	90.8	91.5	92.0	91.1	91.1	91.1
External Causes							
Motor vehicle accidents	2.3	3.1	3.1	2.9	3.6	3.5	3.0
Other accidents	5.9	3.6	3.2	3.1	3.2	3.1	3.4
Suicide	1.9	2.2	2.0	1.8	1.8	1.7	1.7
Homicide	.2	.3	.2	.2	.3	.6	.8
Total	10.3	9.2	8.5	8.0	8.9	8.9	8.9
Total All Causes ..	100.0%	100.0%	100.0%	100.0%	100.0%	100.0%	100.0%

*Includes those causes not specified. A small number classified as "war deaths" is included in "other diseases" in the data for 1960 and 1965; in other years this category is excluded. If "war deaths" were included in the 1974 data, this category would be .04% of the resulting distribution.

Source: Institute of Life Insurance

these are good investments. Thus, insurance companies make money in two ways—one on sales, another on investments. Your wife may ask why you should turn your money over to another so that he can invest it and make more money on it. Why not do it yourself?

You can tell her that if you are paying $600 or so a year for the family's insurance program, you cannot provide the same protection against the loss of your income by, for example, investing that $600 in stocks. There inevitably will be discussion over how much money you should spend each year on insurance and how you can make intelligent use of your cash for both insurance and asset building.

But the central fact remains: life insurance gives your family the kind of financial protection you can get no other way; it provides, when needed, an "instant estate."

How to make insurance work for you

If you and your wife consider insurance as an overall plan, adaptive to various stages in your family's life, you will be able to make good use of the protection. One way to go about this is to anticipate your family's needs at particular points in time. Be sure to bring your wife in on the reasoning. She may have specific views about the family's needs. She also may have to utilize some of the same techniques with her own insurance program when she is a widow.

Start by figuring out how much your family probably would spend a year without your presence. Be sure to include housing, food, clothing, entertainment, vacations, education, transportation, repairs, insurance, and out-of-pocket expenses. Then, determine what money will be coming in each month. What about Social Security, for instance? Be sure your wife understands that if widowed she will receive payments as long as there are dependent children at home or in school, but payments stop after that until she reaches retirement age (see Chapter 5). To find out exact payments due, ask your local Social Security office for a "request for statement of earnings" card. When you mail this to the headquarters in Baltimore, you will find out exactly what your wife would get if you were to die tomorrow.

Will you have a pension? Are there income-producing investments in your estate? Does your wife work? If so, include her salary in the figuring. (Re-

member, though, that you might want to see that
she can quit or cut down on work to take care of
the youngsters. It might be best to figure monthly
income both with and without her salary.)

The difference between what your widow can
expect to receive each month and what her costs are
likely to be is the amount to be covered by insurance. In later years, as your assets grow and your
family needs change, your insurance needs will
change too. It is important to do this kind of reas-
sessing periodically.

Fortunately, many of your insurance needs are
of relatively short duration, and it is possible to
buy limited-time insurance at low cost for those
years when you need extra insurance—while your
children still are at home, for instance. Your wife
should learn that there are two basic kinds of insurance—*term* and *ordinary life,* also called straight
life, whole life, and cash value insurance.

Term insurance is "pure" insurance, paying a
stated amount of money in event of your death. As
its name implies, term insurance covers a specific
length of time. It is "pure" insurance because, like
fire insurance, it pays only in the event of misfortune and is not combined with the savings features
characteristic of ordinary life policies. Typical
terms run for five or ten years, at which time the
policy expires and your protection ends. Often you
can renew the policy without having to take a new
medical exam to prove you continue to be a good
insurance risk, but the premiums will be higher.
Convertible term is a form of term insurance that
can be changed into an *ordinary life* policy within
certain time limits and without need for a physical
exam at that time. Premiums will be raised considerably with the conversion, but the new policy

will offer the advantage of building cash value.

Usually, you cannot continue any term policy after age sixty-five. However, term insurance is perhaps the least expensive protection you can find. For most people, it is a special tool for meeting specific needs that exist for specific periods of time. For some people, term insurance provides the backbone of their protection.

The second type of insurance—*ordinary life*—may cost more than term because of the savings factor built into it. Part of the premium money you pay is returned to you indirectly in the form of a "cash value" if you cancel the policy. You can borrow against the cash value at reasonable interest rates, but your insurance coverage is diminished by the amount of the loan and interest outstanding. A typical $10,000 straight life policy taken out by a man at age thirty-five will cost $190 annually. After ten years it will have a cash value of $1,370 and after fifteen years, $2,350.

Ordinary life is a permanent insurance; premiums do not increase with age, and you can continue your insurance for life without any physical examination other than the one you take to get the policy in the first place.

Tell your wife that premiums usually are figured on so-much-per-thousand dollars of insurance. In most cases, the cost-per-thousand decreases as the size of the policy increases. Women pay less than men, since the statistical odds are that women will live longer. Typically, a woman aged thirty-eight will pay the same premium for the same policy as a man aged thirty-five, for example.

When it comes to comparing the policy of one

What life insurance costs

company with that of another, your wife should be aware that many factors come into play. For one thing, there are two kinds of life insurance companies. These are the *stock companies* and the *mutual companies,* and premiums are figured differently for each. A stock life insurance company is owned by its shareholders; profits are distributed to them. Mutual companies have no stockholders. Instead, they are owned by their policyholders, who receive dividends at the end of most years. These dividends are a rebate representing the difference between premium payments and the actual costs of running the company during that year. You may withdraw your dividends as cash, allow them to accumulate at interest with the company, or use them to buy paid-up insurance in addition to the policy you already have or term insurance with that company.

Policies that pay dividends to policyholders are called *participating* (or "par") policies. Those that do not pay dividends are *non-participating* ("non-par"). Usually premiums are higher with participating policies, but the cost often ends up being lower, once you figure the dividend rebates.

Also pass on to your wife another tip about costs: if possible, pay insurance premiums annually rather than semiannually or quarterly. You will be paying for the company's paper-processing costs if you arrange for multiple payments. It could cost you several dollars a year extra.

What payout options you have   Although the cost of your insurance is significant, it is not the only factor you should advise your wife to consider. How do you want the insurance to go to your beneficiary, for instance, and which

Average* Amount of Life Insurance
Per Family by State

State	Amount	State	Amount
Alabama	$25,000	Montana	$20,200
Alaska	24,700	Nebraska	26,700
Arizona	26,300	Nevada	25,900
Arkansas	16,100	New Hampshire	23,300
California	23,300	New Jersey	31,100
Colorado	26,600	New Mexico	22,100
Connecticut	32,900	New York	27,200
Delaware	40,200	North Carolina	23,300
D.C.	38,800	North Dakota	22,300
Florida	20,800	Ohio	27,900
Georgia	27,100	Oklahoma	21,400
Hawaii	38,100	Oregon	20,400
Idaho	20,900	Pennsylvania	26,200
Illinois	30,100	Rhode Island	26,100
Indiana	26,400	South Carolina	23,800
Iowa	25,200	South Dakota	21,200
Kansas	24,400	Tennessee	24,100
Kentucky	19,900	Texas	26,500
Louisiana	24,200	Utah	24,900
Maine	20,600	Vermont	22,400
Maryland	26,800	Virginia	27,700
Massachusetts	25,700	Washington	20,300
Michigan	30,300	West Virginia	18,800
Minnesota	25,500	Wisconsin	24,900
Mississippi	17,700	Wyoming	24,100
Missouri	25,000	Total U.S.	$26,500

*Total amount of insurance of various kinds divided by total number of families in 1974.

Sources: Institute of Life Insurance, U.S. Department of Commerce

policies offer the best and most economical setup for executing your wishes?

Assuming your wife is your beneficiary, she should know that there are several ways she can collect on your insurance. You can stipulate the method of payment when you buy the policy. If you do not stipulate payment methods, your wife can make specific arrangements with the company after your death.

The most common method of payment is in a *lump sum*. This method works well when you want the policy to provide cash for death and estate-settling costs, for example. Or you and your wife may be satisfied that she can make better investment and nest-egg use of the money herself, rather than have someone else oversee it. On the other hand, you might prefer that the lump-sum payment go directly into a trust fund. A trust could offer both estate tax advantages and the administrative security of having a trusted associate, such as your banker or lawyer, manage the money for your family.

If you do not want the lump-sum arrangement, a number of ways exist for the insurance company to spread out payment of the proceeds. In whatever manner life insurance money may be paid, it cannot be attached by creditors.

Here are some possibilities for regular payment plans to discuss with your wife:

The proceeds can be left with the company so that your widow gets *only the interest*. You also can arrange for her to be able to withdraw more funds, if necessary. This interest arrangement works best only when your widow does not need much money from the insurance, or you wish the bulk of the funds to go to someone else eventually.

Then, there are installment arrangements involving the entire face amount of the coverage. Your widow can be paid a certain sum of money regularly for a *fixed period of years,* for instance. If she dies before that period is finished, payments may continue to your alternate beneficiaries. You can decide in advance how long you want the period to be—perhaps through your children's college years. Payment amounts depend upon the policy's face value, the interest rate guaranteed on the policy, and the time period you select.

By way of example, show your wife what $1,000 would give in monthly installments for various time periods, figured at an interest rate typical of many companies:

Monthly payments for a fixed period

Number of years	Monthly installments per $1,000 of insurance proceeds
1	$84.65
5	18.11
10	9.83
15	7.10
20	5.75
25	4.96

Let's assume your youngest child will have finished college in another ten years. You might buy a $10,000 straight life policy now and arrange to have the proceeds paid to your widow in monthly installments for ten years. If you were to die tomorrow, she would receive approximately $100 a month until all your children were through with school. A similar five-year arrangement would pay her $181 a month.

If you are still alive when your youngest child

has finished school, you might want to change the
policy for other needs. You could use the cash value
to buy additional paid-up insurance. Or you might
switch to some other options that would provide
income adapted to your wife's—and possibly your
—needs now that the children are not dependent.

Instead of a fixed period of time, you might
choose a *fixed-amount option*: your widow would
receive a stipulated sum of money each month until
the principal and interest ran out. Under this arrangement, she usually could change the amount if
she wished.

Then explain to your wife that there are various
life-income options, called annuities. These provide
that a regular sum will be paid to you or other
named persons for the rest of your lives, or for a
specified period. The amount of each installment
depends on the interest rate and the age and sex of
the annuitants.

You can buy a *straight life annuity* that pays an
income to the annuitant (possibly you or your
wife) for life, with no money going to anyone else
if the annuitant dies. You also can buy a *life annuity with installments certain,* which will pay a
specified balance to your beneficiary in case you
should die before a certain time period. A variation
on this arrangement is the *installment-refund annuity.* This also pays you an income for life, but if
you die before you have received as much money as
you put in, the income payments will continue to
your beneficiary until that sum is reached. Or you
could arrange to have the balance paid in a lump
sum, with a *cash-refund annuity.* There also is the
joint and survivorship life-income option. Income
is guaranteed to either beneficiary as long as one
is alive.

You and your wife might look into *variable life* insurance, a new concept designed to withstand the ravages of inflation. Here is how these policies will work when they become generally available.

Currently, in order to meet their payout contract with you, the insurance companies make basically conservative, steady-income investments. With variable life insurance, your premiums would be invested in securities that hold some promise of greater appreciation in value. If those stocks go up in value, the face amount of your policy would also go up. If the stocks go down, so would the face value—but you are guaranteed at least the minimum face value you started with, even if the actual portfolio value drops beneath that amount.

It is a significant concept. Let's say you had bought a $10,000 straight life policy back in 1950. By 1972, that $10,000 would have only $5,900 worth of purchasing power. In contrast, if you had been able to buy a $10,000 variable life policy in 1950, its face value could theoretically have risen to $16,710, assuming the stocks in which your money was invested had risen at the same rate as the Standard & Poor's *Index* of 500 stocks over the same period. This figure also allows for a small yearly deduction for management expenses. Your $16,710 would purchase what $9,900 would have bought in 1950—only a $100 loss from your policy's original face value.

The relative merits of the two basic kinds of insurance are constantly debated by insurance salesmen and financial experts.

These are some of the arguments made for straight life: You have full protection while build-

Minimum Payoff on Variable Life Insurance

Under Securities and Exchange Commission rules, proceeds of variable life insurance cannot be less than the annual premium multiplied by an "age" factor. To illustrate:

Age When Policy Is Bought	Minimum Death Benefit Per $100 of Annual Premium
Under 6	$8,000
6 to 10	$7,100
11 to 15	$6,300
16 to 20	$5,500
21 to 25	$4,700
26 to 30	$4,000
31 to 35	$3,300
36 to 40	$2,700
41 to 45	$2,100
46 to 50	$1,500
51 to 55	$1,300
56 to 60	$1,100
61 to 65	$ 900
66 to 70	$ 800
71 and over	$ 700

Source: *U.S. News & World Report*

ing cash values. You can borrow against that cash value (but you must pay interest in borrowing your own money and the face value of your policy is diminished by the amount of debt that is outstanding at the time of your death). The premiums, unlike those for term policies, can be kept "level" instead of increasing as you grow older.

However, a very strong case can be made for term insurance. You might call your wife's attention to this hypothetical example which appeared in *New York* magazine:

Suppose you and your wife are each thirty-five years old and you have two children, aged eight and six, and an income of $24,000 a year. If you were

An Example of Variable Life Insurance

Assume that at the beginning of 1950, at age 35, you were able to buy a $10,000 variable life insurance policy, and the stocks in which your premiums were invested increased in value at the same average rate as Standard & Poor's index of 500 stocks. Allowing a deduction of ¾ of 1 percent annually for management expenses, here is how the payoff value would have grown in 22 years:

End of Year	What Policy Would Pay At Death	End of Year	What Policy Would Pay At Death
1950	$10,000	1961	$17,210
1951	$10,052	1962	$14,310
1952	$10,880	1963	$16,310
1953	$10,290	1964	$18,730
1954	$12,630	1965	$18,310
1955	$16,350	1966	$17,190
1956	$16,860	1967	$18,820
1957	$15,290	1968	$18,720
1958	$14,410	1969	$16,920
1959	$17,350	1970	$14,030
1960	$15,050	1971	$16,710

Source: Submitted at Securities and Exchange Commission hearings by Aetna Variable Annuity Life Insurance Company

to die, your wife would get around $570 a month from Social Security until your oldest child had reached age eighteen (or age twenty-two, if he stayed in college and remained unmarried). Then she would receive $490 a month until the younger child reached age eighteen. If the child stayed in school until age twenty-two, he would continue to get payments. But your wife would receive nothing more until age sixty. Actually, Social Security payments might be more, under the revised law.

It is quite possible that your widow would need another $1,000 a month for quite a while, once you figure out all her living expenses, including housing, food, medical, transportation, education, insur-

ance, utilities, vacations, and out-of-pocket expenses. Your youngest child won't finish college for
another sixteen years. That $1,000-a-month gap
adds up to $192,000. And *that* would cost you about
$3,000 a year, if you were to cover yourself with
straight life insurance.

If you bought five-year renewable term instead,
your cost would be about $900 to begin with. But
five years from now, it could be $1,200 a year, and
the cost continues to go up with each five-year period. On the other hand, you could buy decreasing
term for $520 a year, setting it up so that coverage
decreases as the children grow and the need lessens.
In fact, you could do all this for even less, because
money earns money over a period of time. Buy only
$159,000 worth of decreasing term (the cost: $430
a year), and even if you were to die immediately,
the $159,000 plus its earnings in a typical bank ac-
count would pay $1,000 a month for sixteen years.

But what about estate taxes, with such a big insurance payoff? There's no question that $192,000
in insurance could well push your estate over the
tax-exempt mark, so your widow would not have
all that money to provide the income she needs.
There is one simple solution, if you handle it correctly: make your wife the owner of the policy.
You can do this by having her take it out on your
life, or you can make a gift of it if you currently
own it. (Ask your lawyer or certified public accountant about gift tax complications, however.)

Be very careful about how premiums are paid
when your wife owns the policy. Otherwise, the tax
courts may decide you actually paid them, and thus
the money could be seen as part of your taxable
estate. To avoid this problem, have your wife pay
the premiums out of her own, separate bank ac-

count. Best of all, if she works, have her put at least part of her pay into a separate account and see that she pays the premiums from that.

In order to establish her clear ownership, you must give up all rights to the policy. That means you cannot change the beneficiary or the settlement terms. (If it were a straight life policy, you could not have access to the cash value, nor could you borrow against it.)

Be sure your wife fully understands all these rules. And that she also understands it could be a wise technique for her to use with her own insurance after you die—by putting the policy into your child's name, for instance.

Insurance provides tax breaks

Although there can be problems with estate taxes, your wife needs to know that insurance does provide some good breaks with income taxes. Life insurance proceeds generally are exempt from federal and state income taxes for the beneficiary, for instance, even though the lump-sum settlement may be much more than the premiums you had paid. In many states, the inheritance tax laws also give favorable treatment to the proceeds from life insurance.

If your insurance provides annuity income, only the interest is subject to income taxes, and that is leveled over the entire life of the annuity. Furthermore, if the surviving spouse is to get the proceeds through an annuity income, there may be a federal tax exclusion of up to $1,000 of taxable interest.

Finally, as the cash value of your policy grows, you are not taxed unless you withdraw it and the money is more than you paid in premiums. Only the excess is taxable.

If you decide to focus on term rather than straight life insurance, you should impress this fact on your wife: the argument for term over straight life requires that the difference in premiums would be used for prudent investment in steady, income-producing sources, such as a combination of savings accounts, bonds with high yields, and possibly a mutual fund with a withdrawal plan (see Chapter 8). Hopefully, these all would provide some hedge against inflation, whereas most kinds of life insurance do not make such provision, simply because they contract to pay a fixed amount in today's dollars, and tomorrow's dollars will buy less.

However, you are right back to the basic problems of money management. Are you and your wife disciplined savers and intelligent investors? Will you really use that premium difference systematically to build a nest egg? Or will you fritter it away in odds and ends for current needs? It is true your insurance needs will diminish as you grow older and your children become independent. But taking the decreasing-term approach demands that you build up assets for your own security in other ways. Many people are not that disciplined. For them, a core plan of straight life (for its savings factors) plus creative use of term policies at various times of need may make the most sense.

CHAPTER 5

Social Security: What Will She Get?

When planning insurance protection for members of your family, you and your wife must know what other income the family will have if you die. A key portion is likely to be Social Security payments. Yet, despite its importance to most families, Social Security can be a most confusing system.

The financial columnist of a leading newspaper reports that questions about Social Security rank at the top of the list of economic questions in his mail from baffled readers. Here are some typical situations he cites:

A middle-aged widow became panic-stricken when her checks suddenly stopped coming. She did not realize that because her youngest child had reached age eighteen and was not continuing in school, all benefits ceased. This situation would continue until she became sixty years old, when she would be eligible to receive widow's benefits in a reduced amount. Even if her child had gone on to college full time, she would lose her portion of survivor's benefits until age sixty. The son would continue to receive some money, however, until he reached age twenty-two—provided he remained in school and did not marry.

A sixty-six-year-old woman, recently widowed, wondered why she had not begun to receive her checks. The answer was that she had not been told she had to file a claim to get the money. She supposed the government would send her payments automatically.

A widow who had been receiving Social Security payments decided to go back to work part time as an executive secretary. She enjoyed the job and agreed to work extra hours. But then she was caught in the dilemma of having to cut back on those hours or forfeit some of her Social Security payments. Similarly, a youngish widow returned to work once the younger of her two children started school. It was a full-time job, and her Social Security check was reduced immediately, although payments for the children continued.

Then, there was the lively lady who after a few years of widowhood met a charming widower in the retirement community where she maintained a small home. Her deceased husband had earned income in high brackets throughout his career. She had at first received 82.5 percent of his benefits monthly and recently had begun to draw 100 percent due to a new provision for widows over age sixty-five. Her current love was also receiving top retirement payments.

Their romance had blossomed to the point of marriage when for the first time they realized they would be forfeiting a considerable sum in Social Security benefits. As his wife, she could receive only an amount equal to one-half his payments rather than the full payments she had received on her deceased husband's earnings record. That meant losing quite a bit of money each month in benefits. The hard economics of the situation led these two to live together without benefit of marriage—the "modern" solution, perhaps, but an unhappy one for many people.

Extremely complex system

And so the stories go, crying for clarification and for just distribution of funds. The fact is it is difficult for anyone short of an expert to figure out how the overall system works, or what specific individuals in specific circumstances will receive.

Yet, that is precisely what concerns you and your wife. What can she count on, and for how long, if you should die when your children are young? What will there be for her once they have left home? What will she receive during her old age? What if she has worked or continues to work? What if she remarries?

Social Security is an extraordinarily complex and comprehensive system. It is not solely a plan for retirement, as many people think. Actually, it embraces four major areas; outline them to your wife:

1. Social Security is an annuity plan for your retirement years.

2. If you die, Social Security provides assistance to your widow and minor or disabled children, and in certain cases your dependent parents.

Federal Spending for Elderly Soars

In 1970, outlays for the elderly—Social Security, Medicare, federal retirement and other benefits—accounted for 19 cents out of each dollar of federal spending. By 1975, outlays for the elderly amounted to about 25 cents of each dollar of federal spending.

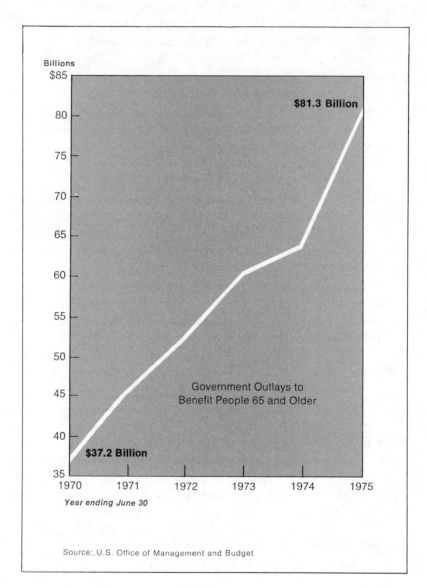

Billions

$81.3 Billion

Government Outlays to
Benefit People 65 and Older

$37.2 Billion

Year ending June 30

Source: U.S. Office of Management and Budget

3. Social Security protects your family if you become totally disabled and cannot work.

4. Social Security provides economic assistance for hospital bills and, if you choose, many medical costs.

This chapter concentrates on what Social Security provides for retirement and survivor benefits, as well as disability payments, since they may apply to your wife if she has been working, too. The medical aspects of Social Security are discussed in Chaptor 6.

How do you know you are qualified?

Whether or not Social Security benefits are payable to a worker, or to his or her survivors, depends upon many factors: the worker's age, earnings, years employed that were covered by Social Security, size of family, age of children and spouse, type of benefit received.

First, there is the question of whether an individual is eligible at all. (The vast majority of workers are.) Eligibility depends upon a system of quarter-year units of work. You are credited with a quarter-year if you have been paid $50 or more in wages covered by Social Security during a three-month calendar quarter. You can be fully insured, in terms of the total credits you have under Social Security; or currently insured, meaning you have one and one-half years' credit within the three years before you die, become disabled, or retire. If you change to a job that is not covered, the credits you have earned will remain on your record. No one is fully insured with credit for less than one and one-half years of work and no one needs more than ten years to be insured in full. There are special provisions for people born before a certain date, which can be checked out with the local Social Security office.

Work credits determine whether or not a person is entitled to Social Security at all. How much they are entitled to depends on what their average earnings have been over the years.

How you figure your benefits

Even though this book is about widowhood, it is important to understand the system by which benefits go to *any* worker eligible under Social Security. Your wife may have worked and earned her own benefits, for instance. She may go to work after you die and begin building up credits. Her status under Social Security regulations may change. What's more, any future planning unfolds best when it is optimistic. Your discussions of what will happen if you die should countenance also what will happen if you live. Any study of your Social Security situation should involve plans for your retirement together as well as thoughts about survivor's benefits.

To find out your maximum benefit and that for your survivors, review your past employment record. If your wife is working, have her figure her own rate base from employment, too, since it is possible that her work record may entitle her to more benefits as a retired or disabled worker than as a widow or wife of a retired worker. Even if that is not the case—and it probably is not, since men usually make more money than women—the calculations will help her learn to untangle the complexities of Social Security.

What a worker must figure is his Average Monthly Earnings (AME) over a stipulated period of time. Here's how you or your wife would determine your AME for your retirement benefits:

1. Calculate your average earnings during your

working years. The number of years of employment you must count depends on the year in which you were born:

Years of Employment

Year of Birth	Number of Years to Count	
	Men	Women
1909	18	15
1910	19	16
1911	19	17
1912	19	18

Beginning with 1913, the number of years to count for men and women are the same:

1913	19
1914	20
1915	21
1916	22
1917	23
1918	24
1919	25
1920	26
1921	27
1922	28
1923	29
1924	30
1925	31
1926	32
1927	33
1928	34
1929 on	35

2. List your earnings for each year from 1951 to the present. Include only earnings from jobs or self-employment covered by Social Security. Don't list any earnings above the Social Security tax ceiling for that year. The maximum earnings to count for each year are:

1951-54	$3,600
1955-58	$4,200
1959-65	$4,800
1966-67	$6,600
1968-71	$7,800
1972	$9,000
1973	$10,800
1974	$13,200
1975	$14,100
1976	$15,300

3. Estimate your expected annual earnings from now through the year *before* you will be sixty-five. Don't list expected earnings above $15,300, the 1976 tax ceiling.

4. Cross off the list those years in which your earnings were (or will be) lowest until the number of years remaining is the same as the number of years you must count in figuring your average (step one). If there were some years you did not work, it may be necessary to include them in your calculations by writing down $0.00 for that year.

5. Add up your earnings for those years, and divide the total by the number of years you must count. The result is your average yearly earnings.

6. Divide your average yearly earnings by twelve to find out your Average Monthly Earnings (AME). This is the guideline you will follow on Social Security tables such as those in the appendix to discover what the benefits will be.

(*Note*: Because the taxable ceiling has been raised several times in the last few years, it is likely to take a number of years, working at top salary range, for your Average Monthly Earnings to equal the top benefit category on any table currently published by the Social Security Administration.)

This specific example will help you determine

your own retirement-benefits AME: Say you were born in 1915, and you plan to retire at age sixty-five, in 1980. To estimate what your retirement benefits will be, put down your earnings, up to the ceiling, from 1951 through 1975. Then list what you expect to earn each year from 1976 up to, but not including, 1980. Suppose these are the figures:

Earnings 1951-1975

1951	$3,600	1963	$4,800
1952	$3,600	1964	$4,800
1953	$3,600	1965	$4,800
1954	$3,600	1966	$6,600
1955	$4,200	1967	$6,600
1956	$4,200	1968	$7,800
1957	$4,200	1969	$7,800
1958	$4,200	1970	$7,800
1959	$4,800	1971	$7,800
1960	$4,800	1972	$9,000
1961	$4,800	1973	$10,800
1962	$4,800	1974	$13,200
		1975	$14,100

Estimated earnings 1976-79

1976	$15,300
1977	$15,300
1978	$15,300
1979	$15,300

Turn to the Years of Employment chart (step one). You will see that you must count twenty-one years when figuring your average yearly earnings. Since you have listed twenty-nine years of earnings, you are allowed to drop eight years from your calculations. The twenty-one years in which your earnings were highest were 1959 through 1979.

Adding up these twenty-one years, you will arrive at a total of $186,300. Next, divide $186,300 by twenty-one to find your average yearly earnings:

$8,871.43. Then divide that number by twelve to find your Average Monthly Earnings, or AME: $739.29.

Suppose you had been sick and could not work during 1959 and 1960. You then would have had no taxable wages during those years. You could re-figure your earnings by dropping 1959 and 1960, replacing them with 1957 ($4,200) and 1958 ($4,200). This would still give you twenty-one years of earnings, totaling $185,100. This figure divided by twenty-one would give you an annual average of $8,814.29, and an AME of $734.52.

To find out what benefit payments your family would receive if you were to die or become totally disabled in 1976, you would figure your AME through 1975 only. Do this by listing your wages from 1951 through 1975, subtracting the five least productive years (just as you did with your retire-ment AME), totaling the remaining wages, and dividing the sum by twenty (the number of years from 1951 through 1975, minus five). That gives your average annual earnings, and by dividing by twelve you find your AME.

If you are younger—say you became twenty-one after 1951—you would have counted the number of years from that birth date instead of from 1951.

How benefits vary   Determining your AME is crucial, because from it you will be able to find out on Social Security ben-efits tables what you and your family would receive under several different circumstances. The figure to look for then is your Primary Insurance Amount (PIA). This is the amount payable each month if you were to retire at age sixty-five or were to die or become disabled prior to that time. The amount is listed on tables after the appropriate Average Monthly Earnings figure, under the category, "Retired Worker (sixty-five or older) ; Disabled Worker (under sixty-five)." Most other Social Security payments are figured in terms of your PIA.

For example, if you wait to retire at age sixty-five, you will get the maximum benefits due in terms of your AME. Suppose you want to collect retirement benefits earlier. You can start as early as age sixty-two, but you will get a reduced benefit for the rest of your life. The reduction will be to 80 percent of your full PIA. If you retire at sixty-three, the percentage is $86\frac{2}{3}$ percent of your full age-sixty-five benefits ; at age sixty-four, it is $93\frac{1}{3}$ percent.

Appendix I is a table showing what you would get if you retired at ages sixty-two and sixty-five, or if you became disabled. Similar figures apply to your wife if she has worked and chooses to take her worker's benefits. (Actually, her benefits as a worker will be slightly higher if she retires between 1973 and 1978. Beginning with retirement in 1978, the amounts will be exactly the same for both sexes.)

The benchmark figure of your retired worker's benefits is important to your wife for several reasons and she should be fully aware of them.

First, her "aged widow's benefits"—if she is sixty or older and there are no minor children in her care—are pegged to your earnings if she has no work record herself. If she starts collecting as a widow at age sixty, she will get 71.5 percent of your age-sixty-five benefits. There is an increased proportion of 5.7 percent a year the later she decides to start collecting: 82.9 percent at age sixty-two, for instance, and 88.6 percent at age sixty-three. If she starts at age sixty-five, she will get the full benefit you would have received, thanks to 1972 revisions

in the Social Security law. The only way she can collect earlier than age sixty, if there are no minor
children in her care, is if she becomes disabled; in
that case, she can receive 50-percent benefits starting at age fifty.

Second, if your wife has a work record of her
own, she will be entitled to her own retired worker
benefits. A woman worker has the choice of receiving her own worker's benefits or those of a widow
or wife, which are pegged to her husband's record.
In fact, she could take her own worker's benefits
starting at age sixty-two—perhaps you still would
be working—then switch to a wife's benefits when
you retire. In this case the wife's benefits will be
slightly reduced, however. This is important to
know because many women have worked only
sporadically, and they forget they have built up
their own Social Security record which they may
collect. Remember, anyone born in 1929 or later
who has paid the tax for at least ten work years—
regardless of when—is eligible.

Third, your AME dictates how much your widow
and children will get if you should die when your
youngsters are still dependents. If your widow is
under sixty-two and there are young or disabled
children in her care, she will get 75 percent of your
full benefit until the youngest child reaches age
eighteen. Each of your children is entitled to 75
percent of your age-sixty-five pension until he
reaches twenty-two, provided he is in school and
does not marry. Benefits to a child disabled before
age twenty-two continue indefinitely.

Under Social Security there is no limit to the
number of members of your family who are eligible
for benefits. Under certain circumstances, you,
your wife, and several children all may collect

monthly benefits. There is, however, a limit to the total that a single family can collect. That limit is called the *family maximum benefit*.

When your family's benefits would add up to more than the allowable family maximum, benefits except those paid to you as the insured worker are reduced proportionately to bring the total down to the maximum set by law. For example, say your average monthly earnings were $500 when you died. If your widow had one dependent child at home, she would receive $485 a month for herself and her child. If she had more than one child, she would get only the $593 maximum set by law. (Figures are rounded off to the nearest dollar.)

Appendix II shows what your widow and your children will receive, depending upon her age and whether or not there are children in her care.

Finally, your wife's receipts when you retire are dictated by your AME, presuming she has no qualifying work record. (Even if she does, your benefits may mean larger checks for her.) If she waits until age sixty-five, she can receive an amount equal to one-half your monthly return. She may choose to draw reduced payments by starting between the ages of sixty-two and sixty-five. She will receive $37\frac{1}{2}$ percent of your benefit if she is sixty-two, $41\frac{2}{3}$ percent if she begins at age sixty-three, and 45 5/6 percent at age sixty-four. All of that is in addition to your retirement check, too, so your household may be receiving anywhere from 137.5 percent to 150 percent of your PIA, if you retire at age sixty-five.

Point out to your wife that if you retire and she is caring for one or more of your dependent chil-

What your wife would receive

dren, she can collect the equivalent of 50 percent of your pension payments. The exception is if she is under sixty-two, there is only one child, and his age is between eighteen and twenty-two, even though he is a student. Again, some rigid family maximums apply.

Let your wife study Appendix III. It shows benefits for you and your wife together when you retire at age sixty-five and she is age sixty-two; when you retire at sixty-five and she also is age sixty-five; and when you retire at sixty-five and your wife and one child qualify for benefits.

Three important stages

As she studies this table she will see that there are three definitive periods for a widow:

• When she is a dependent mother—that is, before her youngest child reaches age eighteen.

• The "widow's gap" period, from that child's eighteenth birthday until the widow reaches age sixty (or fifty, if disabled). This is a period when your widow will receive no benefits for herself, although your children may still be getting some support until age twenty-two, provided they are in school and unmarried. This probably is the best time for your widow to work full time—if there is a choice—because working earlier could mean the reduction or elimination of her dependent mother's payments. Also, the children probably will have left home and she will have more time on her hands.

• Retirement age, with reduced benefits starting at age sixty, and full benefits at age sixty-five, if your widow waits until then.

These basic divisions of time are very important to think about as you plan your estate for your widow.

For the first time in history, Congress in 1972 voted an escalator clause into the Social Security Act. Tell your wife that it works in this way: whenever the Consumer Price Index goes up by 3 percent or more, all Social Security benefits rise automatically by the same percentage. The earliest of these increases was in 1975, and there could be one every year, presuming a yearly inflation rate of at least 3 percent.

What happens with inflation?

If the cost of living goes down—improbable though that may seem—your pension will not be reduced in any way, unless Congress takes some other action.

Explain that all these possible benefits will not come without cost. The wage base ceiling—the top earnings figure, such as $10,800 in 1973, upon which Social Security taxes are determined each year—has risen from time to time over the past years, and it will continue to rise. In 1976, it went from $14,100 to $15,300. Although the rate of taxation did not change then, the Social Security tax percentage may rise in the future, as it did from 5.2 to 5.85 between 1972 and 1973. The maximum tax in 1976 is $895.05 if you are salaried, $1,208.70 if you are self-employed.

The Social Security tax rates probably will continue to rise, even if there is no inflation. If prices and wages do increase, according to the law the wage base must rise, too. Assuming that prices go up 3 percent and wages 5 percent a year, you could be paying $1,444 a year six years from now and $1,894 sixteen years hence. As a matter of fact, assuming those constant inflationary rises per year, according to some experts it is possible that Social Security taxes could go up to $5,344, and all wages up to $73,200 a year would be vulnerable to the payroll tax. Of course, your benefits would skyrocket, too. If you and your wife are thirty years old in 1976 and you retire in the year 2011 at age sixty-five, assuming you make the maximum all along, your monthly check as husband and wife could be $2,729. That's almost $33,000 a year!

Other experts figure it a bit differently, assuming the same 3 percent inflationary rate per year as above. According to those studies, by 1999 the wage base would be more than $40,000, and above $90,000 in 2015, when the maximum tax would be more than $6,500 a year. However, in purchasing power you still would be ahead, despite inflation. According to these experts, your maximum benefits in 2015 would be worth $981 in today's dollars, and that's considerably more than you would get if you retired today.

The table opposite shows what you can expect to have taken out of your salary in future years.

Your wife can work and still collect

Your wife should know that she can earn up to $2,760 a year without losing any Social Security benefits. (That's $2,760 in wages; dividends and other unearned income don't count.) Above that amount, she will lose $1 in benefits for every $2 she earns. However, she can collect her full monthly check during any month in which she earns no more than $230, even though her annual income is over $2,760. Also, none of these restrictions applies once she becomes seventy-two years old.

If your widow remarries

Your wife should be aware that she will lose her Social Security widow's benefits if she remarries, unless she is over age sixty. In that case, presuming

How Your Social Security Taxes Increase*

	1973	1974	1975	1976-77	1978-80	1981-85	1986-2010
Annual Pay	**Tax on Employee & Employer (Each)**						
$ 3,000	$ 176	$ 176	$ 176	$ 176	$ 182	$ 189	$ 194
4,000	234	234	234	234	242	252	258
5,000	293	293	293	293	303	315	323
6,000	351	351	351	351	363	378	387
7,000	410	410	410	410	424	441	452
8,000	468	468	468	468	484	504	516
9,000	527	527	527	527	545	567	581
10,000	585	585	585	585	605	630	645
11,000	632	644	644	644	666	693	710
12,000	632	702	702	702	726	756	774
13,000	632	761	761	761	787	819	839
14,000	632	772	819	819	847	882	903
15,000	632	772	825	878	908	945	968
15,300 and over	632	772	825	895	926	964	987
Annual Earnings	**Tax on Self-Employed Person**						
$ 3,000	$240	$ 237	$ 237	$ 237	$ 243	$ 251	$ 255
4,000	320	316	316	316	324	334	340
5,000	400	395	395	395	405	418	425
6,000	480	474	474	474	486	501	510
7,000	560	553	553	553	567	585	595
8,000	640	632	632	632	648	668	680
9,000	720	711	711	711	729	752	765
10,000	800	790	790	790	810	835	850
11,000	864	869	869	869	891	919	935
12,000	864	948	948	948	972	1,002	1,020
13,000	864	1,027	1,027	1,027	1,053	1,086	1,105
14,000	864	1,043	1,043	1,043	1,134	1,169	1,190
15,000	864	1,043	1,114	1,185	1,215	1,253	1,275
15,300 and over	864	1,043	1,114	1,209	1,239	1,278	1,301

*Total taxes for old-age, survivors, disability, and health insurance (OASDHI).

Note: Tax figures shown for future years make no allowance for automatic increases on higher paid workers as a result of inflation.

Source: Based on Social Security Administration figures

her new husband is collecting benefits, she can choose to collect benefits geared to your income or to her present spouse's. If he were to die, she would switch back to widow's benefits.

Even if her widow's benefits cease because she has remarried, your youngsters will continue to get benefits until the age-eighteen or age-twenty-two-in-school qualifications no longer apply.

What if you divorce?

Generally, Social Security payments to a dependent wife (or husband) cease with divorce. The exception is if your wife is sixty or older and your marriage lasted at least twenty continuous years. Incidentally, your present wife's status with Social Security is not affected by the presence of a previous wife, even though the latter may qualify through your Social Security account, too. Each woman would receive payments under the appropriate conditions.

How the disability benefits work

In general, Social Security disability benefits are equal to the retirement benefits. Explain to your wife that if you become totally disabled prior to age sixty-five ("totally" means severely enough to be unable to maintain a job) and the condition is expected to last for at least twelve months or to end in death, you will receive benefits beginning with the sixth month of your disability. These will continue until you can return to work. Your wife will receive payments equal to one-half of yours if you have a child who is under eighteen or who became disabled himself before age twenty-two. So would each child until he reaches eighteen, or twenty-two if he is a full-time, unmarried student. Again, the family maximum benefit limitation would apply.

These figures are not of as much concern to a widow, unless she is a worker herself and her disability benefits based on her PIA would be more than those received as your widow. The question of her own disability is important in terms of when she can begin to receive retirement benefits. Normally, she could start getting 71.5 percent of the full benefit when she became sixty. However, she could receive 50 percent for the rest of her life starting at age fifty if she became disabled. Also, if there is a disabled youngster in your household, your widow will continue to receive benefits for him even after he reaches age eighteen or twenty-two.

How to protect your Social Security account

You should check on your Social Security account every three years or so. You can find out if your records are accurate by getting a query form from your local Social Security Administration office and sending it to the national headquarters. Your wife should do the same if she has worked.

You each should particularly watch to be sure that your account has been correctly credited for all your income that was taxable under Social Security each year. Pay special attention if you have held more than one job, because your contributions and those of your employers have been sent in from multiple sources.

See that your wife and youngsters get Social Security cards when they start to work. And that they always use their correct numbers when they take jobs; otherwise, they risk not getting credit for all their earnings. If they change jobs, they must make sure their new employers have the correct numbers. Tell them to keep the stubs of their cards in a safe

place in case they lose their cards. Warn them
against applying for a new Social Security number.
If they lose their cards, they should apply for new
cards, not new numbers. If there is a name change
—your wife's changed when she married you, for
instance—the worker should apply for a new card,
not a new number.

Make sure your wife understands that benefits
are not paid automatically; she must file a claim
initially. In addition to getting on the rolls for survivor's benefits when you die, she will receive a
lump-sum payment—up to $255—to help defray
your death costs. (She should receive the money
shortly after she applies for it.) When you plan to
retire, or she plans to retire or to begin receiving a
widow's benefit, file for the benefits at least three
months before the appropriate birthday. That way,
benefits can begin soon after your salary stops or
your widow reaches the qualifying age. You can
receive one year's missed payments retroactively
if you file late, but no more than that. When you
file, you will need your Social Security card, plus
proof of your birth date and possibly your marriage
license. Incidentally, once you reach age sixty-five,
even if you have fibbed about your age in the past or
you intend to go on working full time, be sure to
file. That will bring the government's records up to
date and will put you on the right track for Medicare (see Chapter 6).

If your widow should have any questions about
Social Security benefits, she should contact a Social
Security representative for help. She could call by
phone, or go to the office. Social Security provides
a cornerstone for family income in so many different ways that it is essential she have accurate information and good advice about handling it.

What to Do About Health Care

The most careful plans for your widow's welfare can disintegrate with the costs of a long illness in the family—your own last illness or the illnesses of others after your death—if preparations have not been made to meet such costs. Adequate health insurance is essential for every family.

It is also essential that your wife understand the following: The price of medical care has skyrocketed in the last few years. The cost of a day in a hospital averaged $130 in 1975, compared with $92 in 1972. In large cities the daily charge may be up to 50 percent higher. Physicians' fees have been increasing at a rapid rate too.

One tragedy is that older people, who often live on fixed incomes, are hit with a disproportionate amount of these soaring costs. According to the U.S. Department of Health, Education, and Welfare, people over age sixty-five—representing one-tenth of the population—account for more than one-quarter of the medical spending. In virtually every type of care, the aged have the highest bills. Hospital care costs per person in 1974 for people age sixty-five and over averaged $573, for instance, and only $200 for those between nineteen and sixty-four. Physicians' fees were $182 and $91, respectively; drugs, $103 and $46. These were only *per person* averages for everyone in the defined age groups. You can imagine how much higher were the averages for those who actually were seriously ill.

We may eventually have some sort of national health plan to help defray these high costs. Medicare already fills some of the need for people over age sixty-five, and group insurance obtained at work is helping younger people and their families. However, we cannot count on such aid completely. Despite its general availability, Medicare pays for only about 38 percent of the older population's total medical expenditures, although it does cover about 55 percent of hospital and doctor bills.

Many families simply are not prepared to cope with the bills when a major illness strikes. Often available insurance through work or the government is not enough, and many wives face the double tragedy of watching their husbands die slowly, through a prolonged illness, while the family savings dwindle away on medical bills.

Consider the case of a fifty-five-year-old widowed housewife of Dubuque, Iowa. She had suffered the mental anguish of her husband's terminal cancer for over a year and a half, and had spent more than $22,000 of their own money in medical and hospital

The Rising Cost of Health Care

Total Spending on Medical Care in U.S.

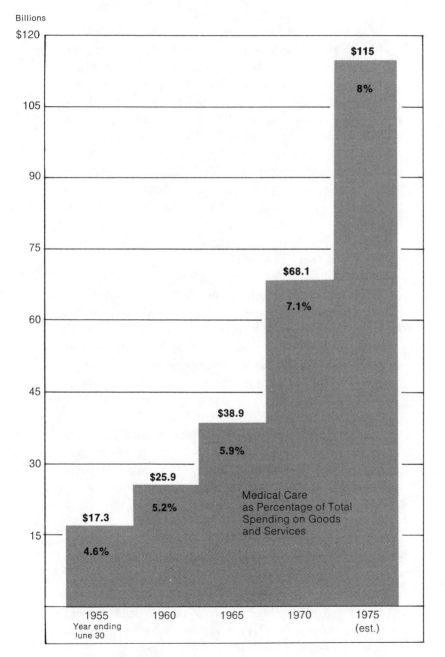

Source: U.S. Department of Health, Education, and Welfare

bills before he died. She was left with less than $1,000 in savings and what remained of a mutual fund to which they had contributed for their retirement. There was only $15,000 in insurance, since they had had to cash in one policy to help pay bills.

This widow's entire life assets were less than $14,000 after she had paid the funeral costs. She was too young to receive Social Security benefits, too old to get a decent job. They had had no children to help with support. Her apartment cost $200 a month, and, although she was able to move into a less expensive one and to find a part-time sales job, her life became a miserable grind of devastated pride and fear about money.

What had gone wrong? They had had a basic medical plan through his employer, but it had not included major medical coverage that is designed specifically to foot the burden of the huge costs that can come with serious illness. The couple went through their medical insurance in a matter of weeks. The remaining expenses had to come out of their own pockets.

Not only a husband's costly illness can wipe out a family's assets; what if the widow herself becomes seriously ill? Unless she has adequate insurance, she is likely to emerge from the sickness with little or no money at all.

Create your health insurance program

Every family should understand all phases of health insurance in detail and create a program that will protect against many possibilities.

Hospital, surgical, and *physician* insurance generally are grouped together in "package plans" sold as one policy. Your wife should be informed that this coverage is provided in two ways:

Health Care and the Elderly

With One-Tenth of the Population, the Aged Account for Over One-Quarter of Medical Spending

	Share of Population	Share of Health Spending
65 and over	10.2%	29.5%
Ages 19-64	55.7%	55.6%
Under 19	34.1%	14.9%

For Practically Every Type of Care, Bills Are Highest for the Aged

Health Spending Per Person in 1974

	65 and Over	Ages 19-64	Under 19
Hospital care	$573	$200	$61
Nursing home	$289	$8	$3
Physicians' services	$182	$91	$57
Drugs	$103	$46	$26
Dentists' services	$20	$37	$19
Other health services	$52	$38	$18
TOTAL	$1,219	$420	$184

Source: U.S. Department of Health, Education, and Welfare

First, *basic insurance,* such as you receive
through Blue Cross/Blue Shield group policies
which cover employed workers. Other companies
sell similar plans to groups and to individuals, and
you can buy individual Blue Cross/Blue Shield as
well, if you don't have group coverage available.

Second, *major medical,* designed to pick up where
basic insurance leaves off. Usually there will be a
specified *deductible*—an amount that must be paid
by you or by your basic insurance before the major
medical insurance begins to pay. And there is a *co-
insurance* arrangement, meaning that you pay 20
percent of the remaining costs, major medical paying 80 percent. Frequently, you will have limits to
the coverage, such as $60 a day for a hospital room,
or $2,000 for a particular operation. Major medical
plans also have maximum dollar amounts. Typical
terms are $10,000 or $20,000 per person per illness
within from two to five years. Even so, your major
medical insurance may pay thousands of dollars
that might otherwise have come out of your pocket.

Usually you can include your family in any group
or individual coverage, although under most plans
your children will be dropped when they reach a
specified age, such as nineteen, twenty-two, or
twenty-three, or when they marry. Then they must
have separate coverage.

Basic and major medical plans vary among companies. You and your wife have some careful shopping to do. Even if you receive all your insurance
coverage through a company plan, you should
check the policies carefully to see if you wish to provide supplements.

Certainly, if you do not have the chance to participate in a major medical plan at work you should
get one on your own.

Rising Health Charges

Increase from 1970 to 1975

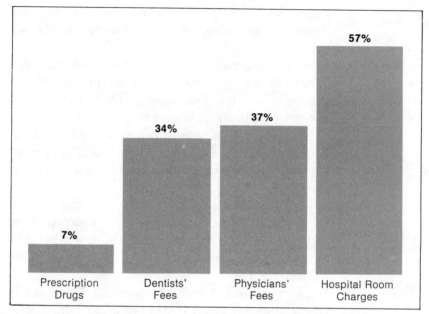

Source: U.S. Department of Labor

You and your wife should keep a number of questions in mind:

What are medical costs in your area? How much are they expected to rise? What plan meets these figures best?

Does the hospital insurance cover such things as private rooms, emergency room treatment, intensive care facilities? How many hospital days are covered? Are payments in full or in part? Are benefits quoted at a flat rate or a percentage? Does the policy cover both illness and accidents? What about nursing care?

Does surgical coverage include postoperative visits by the doctor? An anesthetist's fee? Surgery other than in the hospital?

Will your doctor's bills be paid for office and

Questions to be answered

house calls, or only for care in hospital situations?

How many payments are allowed per family, per person, per year?

With major medical, how much is the deductible? What are the differences in premium costs if you choose to pay the deductible yourself rather than cover it with basic insurance?

How long does any benefit period run? What extras are covered? Can you receive financial help for psychiatric treatment under the major medical plan?

What happens to your family's coverage if you should die or pass a certain age? If you have a physically or mentally incapacitated child, will his coverage stop when he reaches the cutoff age cited for healthy children?

Can your policy ever be canceled? Under what circumstances? What if you are late paying a premium? Can you renew the policy? Can you increase coverage? What if you change jobs or retire; can you convert your group policy to a private plan? Is there a waiver-of-premium clause so your premiums are paid anyway if you become disabled?

No policy is going to give the perfect answer to all these questions. The task is to select the best combination of provisions available to your family.

Disability coverage   You and your wife should consider disability coverage as supplementary insurance. There are disability provisions under Social Security, as mentioned earlier. Disability and rehabilitation benefits may be provided by your state. More and more, auto insurance companies are stressing disability and rehabilitation for victims of auto accidents. Even some installment loans offer coverage. And disability provisions are included in many life insurance plans.

Disability income insurance for the breadwinner (or breadwinners) is as important as major medical for protecting your assets. Your wife should understand this fact in case as a widow she must support the family with her wages. If she cannot work, she won't be bringing in any money. She will have to pay bills out of reserves or funds that she borrows. The combination of huge medical bills and loss of income can ruin a family.

Again, disability plans differ, so some comparison shopping is wise. There are a number of questions to consider. For one thing, are there sources of income other than a job that might cease with disablement? How long could your family survive without financial disaster if income were to be cut off? What are the exact benefits and when, after suffering the disability, would they begin to come in? What is the terminal date, if any? How disabled must the insured be? Confined to bed or home? Or just unable to work? Are there limits to payments for any one disability? If your wife works, how much would you need to supplant her lost income were she to become disabled?

Mail-order insurance

Your wife should understand that some mail-order plans are perfectly sound, if you need them as supplements to your insurance. Others are cleverly advertised ruses. Not that they won't pay as promised—it's just that the "as promised" is hidden in the small print. Most of these really are "hospital income" plans, even though the word "income" may lead you to think of them as disability plans. All they do is pay a certain amount per day while you are in the hospital, usually after a certain period of time.

One catch: Unless it's a good plan (and there are some), payments do not begin until after you have been hospitalized for three days, a week, or even more. Yet the average hospital stay for people under sixty-five is only eight days; for people over sixty-five, it is twelve days. With many of these plans, payments stop as soon as you leave the hospital. The value of such policies is questionable.

Another catch: Many of these plans will not cover you for any illness that begins within a certain time period after signing up. Those that advertise "no medical examination necessary" may not pay when you make a claim; they may declare that you already had an illness or injury when you purchased the policy and that you did not tell them about it.

This is not to say that all mail-order policies are frauds. Just be sure you and your wife know exactly what you are insured against, how much you will be paid, under what conditions, how much you must pay in premiums. If you have any doubts, contact your regional Federal Trade Commission office, the Better Business Bureau, or your state's insurance board before signing up.

Joining Medicare   Your wife should know that there are two parts to Medicare, the over-sixty-five governmental insurance administered by the Social Security Administration. Part A covers hospital insurance. Coverage is free and automatic once you turn sixty-five. Claim payments are not automatic, however; you must file in order to collect. If you become sixty-five after July, 1973, then Part B, which pro-

How Your Medicare Taxes Increase

Year	Maximum Taxable Earnings	Total Tax Rate Divided Equally Between Employee & Employer	Maximum Annual Tax Divided Equally Between Employee & Employer	Tax Rate For Self-Employed	Maximum Annual Tax for Self-Employed
1973	$10,800	2.00%	$216.00	1.00%	$108.00
1974	13,200	1.80	237.60	.90	118.80
1975	14,100	1.80	253.80	.90	126.90
1976-77	15,300	1.80	275.40	.90	137.70
1978-80	15,300	2.20	336.60	1.10	168.30
1981-85	15,300	2.70	413.10	1.35	206.55
1986 and after	15,300	3.00	459.00	1.50	229.50

Note: Tax figures shown for future years make no allowance for automatic increases on higher paid workers as a result of inflation.

Source: U.S. Department of Health, Education, and Welfare

vides some medical coverage, is also automatic unless you say you do not want it. You will pay a monthly premium of a few dollars for the Part B coverage, which is usually deducted from your Social Security checks. (People who became sixty-five before July, 1973, had to sign up for Part B.) Again, you must file to collect a claim.

Most Americans over age sixty-five are eligible for at least part of the Medicare coverage, and many people under sixty-five who became disabled within two years of July, 1973, are also eligible. These include disabled widows aged fifty or over, workers, dependent widowers, and people disabled before age twenty-two.

The over-sixty-five eligibility breaks down according to Part A or Part B. For the hospital insurance, you are eligible if you are entitled to Social Security or Railroad Retirement benefits. (You get Medicare even if you go on working after age sixty-five and do not receive your Social Security payments.) If you became sixty-five before 1968, you do not need full work credits to qualify. And if you do not qualify at all, you can buy the hospital protection on a voluntary basis, currently for about $40 a month. Under those circumstances, when you enroll in Part A you also must sign up for Part B.

Formerly, if you did not sign up for Part B within three years after your first chance or after you had withdrawn from the program, you would lose your eligibility. Now there is no three-year eligibility provision, but your premium will be increased by 10 percent for each full year you could have enrolled but did not. If you turn down or cancel the coverage, you may reenroll during any general sign-up period, from January 1 through March 31 of each year. You can enroll, cancel, and enroll again, but after the second cancellation you forfeit your right to Medicare coverage. Your Social Security office has the details.

Your wife will be eligible, too, when she reaches age sixty-five. She can get the hospital provisions if she is eligible for Social Security benefits on her own work record or as your wife. She will continue to benefit even when she is a widow. She also will receive (and pay for) Part B as your wife or widow, or as a worker—unless she turns it down.

The benefits of Medicare

These are points your wife should learn about Medicare coverage: Under Part A, after you have paid a deductible of $104 on your hospital bill, you will have all normal services covered in a semi-private room for up to ninety days. After the first sixty days, you pay $26 a day of your bill. There is a "lifetime reserve" of sixty more days to help out if you must be in the hospital beyond ninety days for any one stay, or "benefit period." For those extra days, you will pay $52, the government paying the rest.

There are nursing home provisions as well—if you spend three consecutive days in the hospital and are admitted to a nursing home or other Medicare-approved "skilled nursing facilities" within fourteen days after you were discharged from the hospital. The care must be skilled nursing care, not custodial care. After the first twenty days, you will pay $13 a day.

Note: That phrase, "Medicare-approved," is crucial. You are covered only in institutions that have met certain government standards. That goes for hospitals as well as nursing homes, so be sure to check the facility carefully for its eligibility. Especially with nursing homes, many families have been startled to learn they owed the full bill because the home had not been approved by Medicare.

Some "home health care" provisions also are included under Part A. The care must be through a participating agency, like the Visiting Nurse Association. Certain items, such as private-duty nurses, are not covered by the insurance. You must have been in the hospital three days, and home care visits are limited to 100. You are allowed 100 *without* a hospital stay if you have medical (Part B) coverage. Medicare will pay 100 percent of any "reasonable" costs that are incurred. There is a $60 annual deductible.

Part B covers the major portion of any of your physicians' or surgeons' fees for each calendar year. You are covered whether you go to a hospital, clinic, or doctor's office, or if you are treated in your home or elsewhere. You will pay the first $60 of your annual charges, plus 20 percent of the balance.

Under Part B you are covered for a sizable portion of X-rays and surgical dressings, as well as some other services to outpatients. However, you are not covered for eye and ear examinations, routine physical exams, immunization shots, or medication you take yourself.

With all its provisions, Medicare is not enough. Tell your wife that gaps should be filled with supplementary insurance unless you can afford to pay out of your savings. Some possibilities: Your group insurance, if you still work. Converting your group insurance to a private plan when you retire—if the company allows conversion. Group coverage through organizations such as your union or fraternal association.

Also, you can check your Blue Cross/Blue Shield office to see if there is over-sixty-five supplementary insurance available in your area. It could cost you only a few dollars a month for a plan that will pay all the hospital and medical care expenses not covered by Medicare. That includes deductibles and the amounts you pay jointly with the government. Such plans may even contribute somewhat to extended-care-facility costs.

In some parts of the country, for higher premiums you can get a Blue Cross/Blue Shield plan for benefits up to $10,000 or so, including private nurses and drugs. Plans also exist in many areas for senior citizens who are not eligible for Medicare. Commercial companies often offer similar insurance.

One kind pays a certain amount, such as $100, every week of hospitalization after the first week or so, up to fifty-two weeks. You will have to weigh

Hospital Costs Compared

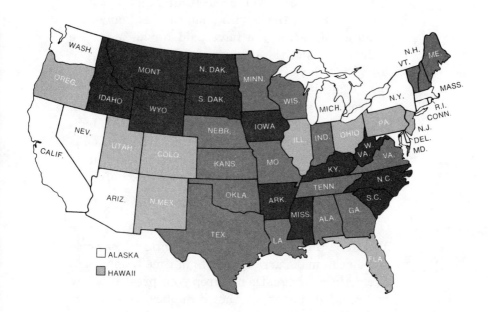

Daily Hospital Expense Per Patient in 1973

 $110 or more

$95 to $109

$80 to $94

Less than $80

Source: U.S. Department of Health, Education, and Welfare

the premium cost per year against the odds of how long you might be in the hospital.

Other policies cover areas that Medicare does not, but look at these with a sharp eye; many contribute only after you have paid for all Medicare deductibles and the government has covered your first sixty days in the hospital. The chances of being hospitalized that long are not great.

Probably your best bet is to find a major medical plan that covers most expenses not paid by Medicare in and out of the hospital. More information is available from the Institute of Health Insurance, 277 Park Avenue, New York, New York 10017.

Supplementary health insurance

As you near age sixty-five, you and your wife should be thinking about supplementary insurance so you can make arrangements in time to maintain adequate coverage. Do not drop your present policy before establishing whether it duplicates Medicare coverage or excludes benefits provided by Medicare.

If your wife is younger than you, she must realize that she will not have Medicare until she becomes sixty-five unless she is disabled or has chronic kidney disease, requiring hemodialysis. You may want to retain your present policy to assure her coverage or buy other insurance for her if your present policy ceases when you become sixty-five.

When briefing your wife, remember to stress that the best medical insurance is preventive health care. That means keeping fit as well as you can through intelligent diet, regular checkups, and exercise.

Increasingly throughout the country, health insurance companies and other institutions are setting up programs for preventive health care. You and your wife might seriously consider such a program if it is available. If you make good health habits a necessary routine in your lives, your chances for fitness—and minimal expense—are naturally improved.

7

Other
Sources
of
Income

Despite recent increases in Social Security payments and the promise of further rises with inflation, Social Security income is not adequate for even modest survival. This makes it essential to provide additional income, especially in situations where there may be a period of years during which children are to be educated and your widow may not be eligible for Social Security benefits.

You and your wife will want to survey a number of sources of additional income which you both can manage while you are together and which she can direct alone at a later date should that be necessary.

If your company or union offers a pension plan, you and your wife should consider several key aspects.

How Private Pension Plans Have Grown

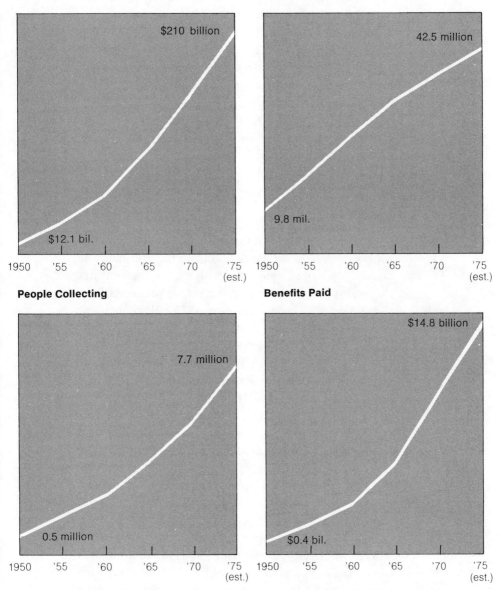

Total Assets

$210 billion

$12.1 bil.

1950   '55   '60   '65   '70   '75 (est.)

Workers Covered

42.5 million

9.8 mil.

1950   '55   '60   '65   '70   '75 (est.)

People Collecting

7.7 million

0.5 million

1950   '55   '60   '65   '70   '75 (est.)

Benefits Paid

$14.8 billion

$0.4 bil.

1950   '55   '60   '65   '70   '75 (est.)

Sources: Institute of Life Insurance, Securities and Exchange Commission, Social Security Administration

How much do you *contribute* each month, and how much does your company put in? Do you have options about this?

When do you become *vested* in the program, and to what extent? In other words, for how long must you have participated in the program before you are entitled to some or all of the company's contributions as well as your own? What happens if you leave the company before you retire?

Is there a *survivor's option?* Does your wife or family get the money if you die? Would they get it if you die before you retire? How long would it continue?

Pension plan problems Ignorance about survivors' options is a frequent source of dismay and disappointment. For example, one couple had planned carefully for retirement and the widow's well-being by including proceeds from the husband's pension plan—$150 a month—in their projections for future security. Along with Social Security and a small mutual fund withdrawal plan, the pension plan rounded out a modest, but comfortable, fixed income. Unfortunately, the husband died just before retirement, and it turned out that the bulk of the pension plan (the part that came from company contributions) was withheld, since he had not fulfilled the time limit imposed in the contract. Another widow missed out altogether on income from her deceased husband's pension plan because he had not signed up for the survivor's benefit. He thought it was automatic.

Despite problems, good pension plans can provide valuable security. Some companies provide contributory savings, profit-sharing, and investment programs in addition to (or instead of) pension plans.

Private Pension Benefits

Length of employment	Median monthly pension for each year of employment for—	
	Men	Women
Less than 10 years	(^{1})	(^{1})
10-14 years	5.30	3.50
15-19 years	4.95	3.40
20-24 years	5.55	3.45
25-29 years	5.60	3.75
30-34 years	6.75	3.75
35-39 years	6.60	
40 years or more	6.10	3.70

[1] Not computed because base less than 2,250.

Source: Social Security Administration survey

These also can offer substantial capital growth over the years, together with tax advantages.

Your bank accounts

Your wife should know that there are a number of different kinds of savings institutions, presenting a somewhat complicated situation. There are commercial banks, for instance—the "full service banks," where you can save, borrow, have a checking account, obtain a bank credit card, often receive trust and estate planning help, and, generally, find a wide variety of banking services. Then there are the savings and loans institutions and the mutual savings banks, which concentrate on mortgage lending and savings accounts. Finally, credit unions are very much in competition with the banks to obtain savings accounts and make consumer loans. You must belong to an affiliated group to use a credit union, however.

Generally, you will get a higher rate of return at the savings banks, the savings and loans institutions, and the credit unions. (You also can get low-cost life insurance at savings banks in New York, Massachusetts, and Connecticut.) However, most commercial banks offer conveniences such as checking accounts, bank cards, and automatic transfer of funds from checking to savings. Many find it expedient to maintain both an account at a commercial bank and a savings account in a savings institution.

Interest figured in many ways
The many different ways interest is figured also create some confusion. Some institutions compound interest daily, others monthly, quarterly, or twice a year. With many banks there is a "grace period," which allows money deposited within a week or ten days of the beginning of the interest period to be treated as though it had been deposited right from the start. Some banks pay you interest on everything in your account from the day of deposit to the day of withdrawal; others figure on the lowest balance in your account during the interest period.

All in all, there are more than a hundred ways to compute interest on savings, according to the American Bankers Association. Senator Vance Hartke has claimed that you could apply the same interest to the same sum over a six-month period and there would be a variance of as much as 150 percent in interest earned, depending upon the method of computation. If you are undecided about where to bank your cash, you might ask the prospective bank to calculate how much you actually would earn in a year, presuming you followed a specific schedule of timing and amount of deposits.

Actually, unless the sum is quite large, the interest method will not make too much difference. The interest *rate*, however, is important. Since the purpose of savings is to build a nest egg, consult the table on page 136, showing specific goals and time periods and how much you should deposit each month at five different interest rates to meet those goals. By current law, the commercial banks are limited to 5 percent interest on regular accounts; savings and loans and savings banks to $5\frac{1}{4}$ percent. The $5\frac{3}{4}$ percent figure is typical of some time deposits, as well as many credit unions. In fact, some credit unions pay up to $6\frac{1}{4}$ percent in good years.

To simplify matters, the table presumes that you make the deposits on the first of each month, the deposits are the same amount each month, and interest is compounded continuously.

The regularity of deposits is very important in any savings program. If you fear you may lack discipline, take advantage of the automatic techniques provided by some banks. They will transfer a specified sum from your checking to your savings account regularly, for instance. Avoid Christmas clubs or travel clubs, however, unless they pay as high an interest rate as do the regular savings accounts.

If you find it easier to figure in terms of what you can afford to save each month, rather than how much you want after a certain time, here is another way to gauge what you can save over the years. The figures on page 137 are determined at 5 percent interest, compounded quarterly.

Achieving Savings Goals by Monthly Deposits

To amass this amount:		Put this aside each month at the interest rate of:				
		5%	5¼ %	5½ %	5¾ %	6%
$2,000 in	1 year	$162.20	$161.98	$161.76	$161.53	$161.31
	3 years	51.39	51.19	50.99	50.78	50.58
	5 years	29.28	29.08	28.88	28.70	28.48
$4,000 in	1 year	$324.40	$323.96	$323.52	$323.06	$322.62
	3 years	102.78	102.38	101.98	101.56	101.16
	5 years	58.56	58.16	57.76	57.40	56.96
$8,000 in	5 years	$117.12	$116.32	$115.52	$114.80	$113.92
	10 years	51.28	50.59	49.90	49.21	48.52
	15 years	29.78	29.16	28.54	27.93	27.31
	20 years	19.36	18.81	18.26	17.72	17.16
$12,000 in	5 years	$175.68	$174.48	$173.28	$172.20	$170.88
	10 years	76.92	75.88	74.85	73.82	72.78
	15 years	44.67	43.74	42.81	41.90	40.97
	20 years	29.04	28.22	27.39	26.58	25.74
$16,000 in	5 years	$234.24	$232.64	$231.04	$229.60	$227.84
	10 years	102.56	101.18	99.80	98.42	97.04
	15 years	59.56	58.32	57.08	55.86	54.62
	20 years	38.72	37.62	36.52	35.44	34.32
$20,000 in	5 years	$292.80	$290.80	$288.80	$287.00	$284.80
	10 years	128.20	126.47	124.75	123.03	121.30
	15 years	74.45	72.90	71.35	69.83	68.28
	20 years	48.40	47.03	45.65	44.30	42.90

Source: American Bankers Association

At the end of this period of time . . .	If you save this amount each month at 5% interest, compounded quarterly			
	$10	$20	$50	$100
	you will have saved this much:			
1 yr.	$ 123.29	$ 246.58	$ 616.44	$1,232.88
5 yrs.	682.53	1,365.06	3,412.65	6,825.30
10 yrs.	1,557.56	3,115.12	7,787.80	15,575.59
15 yrs.	2,679.38	5,358.76	13,396.89	26,793.79
20 yrs.	4,117.59	8,235.19	20,587.97	41,175.95

Time deposits

Time deposits can provide good use of extra funds, once you have put sufficient cash into readily available accounts for emergency access. Bank savings certificates—or certificates of deposit, or "golden" savings accounts, or whatever the particular institution calls them—pay higher interest rates than ordinary accounts because you must leave your money on deposit longer. Typically, the rate is from 5½ percent to 7¾ percent with a time limit of from 90 days to six or more years, depending upon the institution and the plan. In 1973 the government authorized certificates of deposit of $1,000 or more for four years or more with no rate ceiling, but this was rescinded when it affected the amount of money deposited at lower interest.

Savings certificates continue to earn the same interest rate until they mature, even if the prevailing rate drops. The disadvantage is that your money is tied up. If there is an emergency, you can

How to Earn the Most on Savings

Type of Account	Interest Rate Ceiling
In Savings and Loan Associations	
Regular passbook	5.25%
90-day notice	5.75%
90-day CD	5.75%
1-year CD—$1,000 minimum	6.5%
2½-year CD—$1,000 minimum	6.75%
4-year CD—$1,000 minimum	7.5%
6-year-or-over CD—$1,000 minimum	7.75%
In Commercial Banks	
Regular passbook	5.0%
90-day certificate of deposit—no minimum balance	5.5%
1-to-2½-year CD—no minimum	6.25%
2½-year CD—no minimum	6.5%
4-to-6-year CD—$1,000 minimum	7.25%
6-year-or-over CD—$1,000 minimum	7.5%
In Mutual Savings Banks	
Regular passbook	5.25%
90-day certificate of deposit— no minimum balance	5.75%
1-to-2½-year CD—no minimum	6.5%
2½-year CD—no minimum	6.75%
4-to-6-year CD—$1,000 minimum	7.5%
6-year-or-over CD—$1,000 minimum	7.75%

Note: A certificate of deposit is a receipt for money deposited for a certain period of time. CDs of $100,000 or more, whether issued by commercial banks, mutual savings banks, or savings and loan associations, are under no ceiling.

Sources: Federal Reserve Board, Federal Home Loan Bank Board, Federal Deposit Insurance Corporation

submit a written application for withdrawal, but you will lose some interest. Nevertheless, these savings certificates do provide a clearcut way to save a predetermined amount at relatively favorable rates in a defined period of time. For that matter, a 6 percent return on your money may be more than you can get from many securities these days.

Most banks are insured by the Federal Deposit Insurance Corporation, which means that your savings account is fully protected up to $40,000. Actually, you can keep much more in one bank with complete insurance coverage by opening several different accounts: **Is your money safe in banks?**

You and your wife could have a joint account. Each of you could also have your own account. And each of you could have an account in which one is trustee for the other. You can open accounts for your children, too. Thus, a couple with one child could have six separate accounts in one bank, fully insured against loss up to a total of $240,000.

Remember that tying up all your money at the safe rate of 5 to 6 percent may not be the best course when inflation is rampant. Some economists now speak of a 3 or 4 percent rate of inflation each year, but not long ago the inflation rate was almost 6 percent in one year. If your savings then earned as much as 6 percent, they still would not have kept abreast of inflation because taxes took part of your interest earnings. Although a reserve fund in savings accounts may be advisable, the bulk of your assets can be more profitably invested in other ways.

Though banks daily perform many valuable services, the average person seems unaware of some important rules concerning banking operations.

Upon the sudden death of her husband, a widow sought to reassure her brother that she had sufficient cash to tide her over through the settlement of her estate.

"We never had a joint checking account," she said a day or two after the funeral, "but it's all right because John always signed a whole book full of checks." She displayed a book of checks, all signed by John.

The poor woman did not know that the account was frozen from the moment the bank learned of his death. No checks signed by John would be honored—even though they might have been drawn before his death.

Freezing of bank accounts at death is intended to protect the owner—and the tax claims of government. A person who owns a checking account can always change his mind at the last minute and stop payment on a check. The bank therefore acts when the owner of an account no longer is able to do so. Perhaps even more important is the aspect of federal estate taxes, as well as estate or inheritance taxes in those states where they exist. A bank has no way of knowing how large an estate may be, and the government definitely wants to know. The money in a checking account must be listed in the assets of an estate and might be taxable. If there were no bank regulations to prohibit payment of a dead man's checks, a widow could write a check withdrawing all funds from the account, and thereby evade the estate tax.

It is therefore important to have some funds readily available for your wife at all times. Probably, her own checking or passbook savings account would serve this purpose. But by what other means can you and your wife make good use of services banks offer? How can you determine if you are getting the most for your money?

For the most part, U.S. savings bonds are a steady, though unspectacular, way to save. Actually, in the early 1970s U.S. savings bonds yielded an average annual return of 5.5 percent when held to maturity. This was not a bad showing at a time when savings and loan funds averaged 5.3 percent, mutual savings banks 5 percent, and commercial bank savings accounts 4¾ percent. (Note that these are averages; it was possible to get higher returns, depending upon the account and the savings institution, and even the geographic location.)

U.S. savings bonds

U.S. savings bonds offer other advantages. For instance, there are two kinds of savings bonds that work separately yet can be managed advantageously in connection with each other. These are the *Series E bond,* which is a savings bond, and the *Series H bond,* a current-income device.

E bonds are sold at 75 percent of maturity value. If held to maturity (for five years), they pay 6 percent. You can buy a $25 bond for $18.75, for instance, and receive $25.20 after five years; or, you pay $75 to get back $100.80 after maturity. If you redeem the bonds earlier, you receive a lower rate of interest. You can cash them in two months or later after purchase.

E bonds are sold in denominations of $25, $50, $75, $100, $200, $500, $1,000, and $10,000. The most you may buy in one calendar year is $10,000 worth. You and your wife (or someone else) can buy jointly up to $20,000 a year.

An attractive E bond feature is that you can buy

them on a regular basis through a company payroll savings plan. That provides a discipline you might otherwise find difficult to maintain on your own. Another advantage: you can choose to defer payment of taxes on the interest until you cash in the bonds. This opens the way to a number of maneuvers that may suit your family situation, as you will see below.

H bonds sell at par or face value—for example, a $1,000 bond sells for $1,000—and pay interest by Treasury check twice a year. The redemption period is ten years, and the 6-percent-to-maturity rate will be less if you cash the bond in early. The earliest you can redeem an H bond is six months after you buy it. You pay federal income taxes on the interest.

You can buy H bonds in denominations of $500, $1,000, $5,000, or $10,000, with a $10,000 annual limit on the amount you can purchase ($20,000 jointly owned). There is no limit if you convert from E bonds. This conversion possibility provides an opportunity for retirement income for you both or for your widow. If you buy E bonds regularly and defer reporting the interest until you retire, you have two choices for disposing of them:

You can cash in the bonds and pay taxes on the accrued interest. Presumably, your taxes will be less because you earn less in retirement and you are allowed a double exemption.

How bond conversion works

If you want income instead, convert these bonds to H bonds. You will pay no tax on the E bond interest until you or your estate cashes the H bonds. In the meantime, you will receive a regular income twice a year from the H bond interest, and only that amount is taxable. Here are two examples of how this conversion works:

One man bought a $100 E bond a month (for $75 each) through his company's payroll deduction plan for fifteen years and ten months before he retired. His net accumulation: $22,225 for an investment of $14,250. When he retired, he added $275 in cash to get a multiple of $500, and switched to $22,500 in H bonds. For the next ten years, he received a Treasury check for almost $630 twice a year, or about $105 a month, and he still had kept the $22,500 intact.

At that point, he could have cashed in the bonds and paid taxes on the outstanding E bond interest at his reduced retirement tax rate. Or he could have continued the H bond plan, receiving interest once again and preserving the capital for his estate. In fact, he had the bonds listed in his wife's name, too, and when he died, she had access to them immediately, since jointly-owned property is not held up in probate. She was able to cash some to help defray funeral expenses. She could keep the rest to provide income and ultimately pass them on to her children when she died.

Another man invested $10,000 outright in E bonds and kept them for twenty years, by which time the redemption value had risen to $29,599. Then, ready to retire, he exchanged the E bonds for H bonds. Although the ensuing interest income was taxable, he had paid no tax on the $19,599 interest that had built up over his twenty-year ownership of the E bonds, and no tax would be due until the H bonds were cashed by him or his heirs. His income from the H bonds averaged about $1,630 a year, or approximately $135.10 a month.

If he had placed that $10,000 in a savings account

or in an investment earning the same interest, he would have been taxed on the earnings each year, thus having less income to reinvest. Assuming he was in a 25 percent tax bracket, he would have had only $22,628 after twenty years. What's more, savings bonds are exempt from state and local income taxes, so he saved even more by buying bonds.

The Treasury Department also suggests an E bond plan with tax advantages for building up a nest egg to pay for your children's education: Buy the bonds regularly and register them in your youngster's name, with you or your wife as beneficiary rather than co-owner. At the end of the first year, file a tax return for your child in order to report the interest earned on the bonds. This shows the government your "intent" and you do not have to file again unless your child's income exceeds his personal exemption. Even if he does earn more than that, the tax would be less than if you had to pay it in your higher bracket. When your child is ready for college, you can redeem the bonds to help cover expenses, and there will be no tax on the accumulated interest. Be sure to keep a copy of the original tax return you filed for the child.

Despite such advantages, there are some less favorable points about bonds. You are not able to use them as collateral against a loan, for instance. Also, to receive the full 6 percent annual interest, you must hang on to the bonds until their maturity, and—as with all fixed savings—inflation could well have eaten away the gain almost entirely.

Income from real estate   If you own valuable property, such as an apartment house, or if you speculate in real estate, you probably are receiving expert counsel. But have

you involved your wife so that she understands
what is going on? A common form of income-producing real estate is rental from a second home
bought purely for investment and perhaps retirement later on; or from a vacation home that your
family uses as well as rents.

However, recent rulings have eliminated some of
the attractive tax advantages attached to ownership of vacation homes. Let's say you have a ski
cottage that you rent for two months out of the
three-month season for $1,000 a month. Your fam-
ily uses it the other month, and the house is closed
for the rest of the year. Formerly, you could deduct
all your expenses for the period you were renting
the place. If your expenses for that time exceeded
your income, you could claim a business loss on your
personal income tax return. For example, on the
one-third personal use, two-thirds rental basis,
your allocation of expenses might go like this:

Expense item	Total	⅔ portion charged to rentals	⅓ portion charged to your family use
Mortgage interest	$1,200	$ 800	$ 400
Property taxes	600	400	200
Maintenance	600	400	200
Utilities	300	200	100
Depreciation	1,200	800	400
Totals	$3,900	$2,600	$1,300

Since you received only $2,000 in rental income
against an outlay of $2,600, you are out $600 on
your rental operation. Under the old law, you could
claim that $600 as a business loss on your personal
income tax, which could mean a considerable tax
savings, depending upon your income bracket. In

addition, you could deduct the one-third of mortgage interest and property taxes attributable to the non-rental expenses, a total of $600 that you had allotted to your personal use of the home.

Tax law changed   This is no longer the case. The IRS has ruled that any property held for personal use as well as for rental is not primarily a business property. As a result, your expenses will be counted only up to a break-even point—that is, up to the amount of rental income you receive. What's more, you must attribute *all* your mortgage interest and property taxes to the rental, even though you use the place some of the time for family entertainment, not for rental business. Only if the mortgage interest and taxes amount to more than your rental income can you take the difference as a deduction on your personal income tax return.

For the ski house situation above, you would now figure this way: Your rental income was $2,000 and your total interest and real estate taxes were $1,800. That leaves only $200 against which you can deduct all other expenses, including utilities, maintenance, and depreciation. Even if you spent more on utilities and maintenance while the renters were there, you can deduct only $200.

In this case, on your personal tax return you have lost the previous operating-loss deduction of $600, plus the additional deduction of $600 for interest and taxes. If, however, you had received only $1,000 in rental income, you could have counted the additional $800 in taxes and interest as deductions on your personal return.

This change of the law should not dissuade you or your widow from owning a second home for busi-

Sources of Family Income

(Percent of families in each income group in 1974)

Family Income	Total	Earnings Only (Wages and salaries and self-employment income)	Earnings Plus Income Other Than Earnings*	Income Other Than Earnings Only*	No Money Income Reported
Under $3,000	100.0	21.5	32.9	41.3	4.3
$3,000 to $4,999	100.0	16.4	39.2	44.4	—
$5,000 to $6,999	100.0	27.6	45.2	27.3	—
$7,000 to $9,999	100.0	34.0	54.9	11.1	—
$10,000 to $14,999	100.0	34.9	61.3	3.8	—
$15,000 to $24,999	100.0	28.3	70.6	1.1	—
$25,000 to $49,999	100.0	15.5	83.7	0.8	—
$50,000 and over	100.0	11.3	87.1	1.5	—
All families	100.0	23.7	59.4	16.4	0.5

Note: Parts may not add to totals due to rounding.

*Income other than earnings includes Social Security benefits, dividends, interest, rental income, public assistance, unemployment compensation, private pensions, annuities, and alimony.

Source: U.S. Census Bureau

ness reasons. If you do use it for your vacations as well, you will have the pleasure of its use and the probability that it will appreciate in value over the years. In the meantime, you still may be able to defray some expenses. You will get the full mortgage interest and property tax deductions one way or the other, and if you take in enough rent you may gain some advantages from the business depreciation laws, too. Let's say that on that same house you received $2,200 for the two months. Or you rented it for two summer months in addition and took in another $1,000 in income that way. The first possibility leaves $400 against which you can apportion operating costs and depreciation; the second, $1,200.

A vacation home also may serve eventually as a retirement home for you both or for your widow, so it could be a good investment on those grounds despite the tighter tax regulations. If you keep it strictly as a rental property and do not use it for your family except on very rare occasions, you can handle taxes in the old business-profit-and-loss way. You must be able to show the government that you are maintaining the home for profit purposes. It will be considered a business proposition if you can demonstrate an overall profit in two out of the last five years—in which case you would not be deducting losses against your personal income much anyway. If you have recently bought the house or have just decided to use it for income rather than for family purposes, you have five years in which to show a profit for two years. Any tax benefits you received during that time will be forfeitable retroactively if you fail to meet the test. The exception would be if you could convince the IRS that you had failed to show a profit only after a reasonable attempt to make money from the venture. You would have to show evidence that you had advertised it, set a competitive rental rate, and occupied it very little yourself.

Savings accounts, pensions, government bonds, and real estate are ways to provide your widow with steady income to supplement your Social Security and insurance. Of these possibilities, only real estate has a fair chance of appreciating in value at a pace that may outstrip inflation significantly. Once you have a solid core of fixed income assured for your widow, you must also consider ways to invest your assets so that their value keeps pace with, or exceeds, the rate of inflation.

CHAPTER 8

Tell Her About Stocks and Bonds

A Wall Street broker tells this story: A widow in her late sixties had been his client for several years. She had a little money to invest after her husband died, and although she was without previous experience in the stock market, she had managed to amass quite a nest egg over the years.

What confounded her broker was that she did most of the research on her own. Often she turned down his suggestions in favor of an investment of her own choosing. And usually she was right.

As one success followed another, the broker began to believe she was a genius in the investment field. Somehow, that widow managed to spot stocks having not merely moderate growth potential but frequently those which soared in value over a period of time. What's more, she always seemed to know exactly when to sell. He concluded that her knowledge of the market was extraordinary.

One day she came into his office with an order to sell 200 shares of common stock of a relatively new electronics company. The broker did not approve of the transaction particularly, but she insisted, so he put through the order to sell. As they were chatting a bit later, he saw the record of the sale of 200 shares of that stock go by on the ticker tape. Just as a pleasantry, he pointed it out to her, saying, "Somebody just bought your stock. There it goes on the tape now. . . ."

Unexpectedly, she was silent. She looked at him, then at the tape, and back at the broker. "But," she stammered in distress, "but—then that means someone thinks I'm *wrong!*"

In all her years of successful investing, she had been really just lucky. In fact, freakishly lucky for she had never understood how the stock market worked. It had never occurred to her that every time she sold a company's stock, someone else thought the time was right for buying it. And every time she bought a stock, someone else thought the time had come to get rid of it.

Although the process isn't quite that simple, in essence that is what you should tell your wife the stock market is all about. For most transactions that take place, there is a buyer who thinks one thing about a stock and a seller who thinks the opposite. One decides to sell because he thinks he won't gain from then on by holding the stock, or because he thinks it may decline to his loss otherwise, or because he can realize a profit at that moment. The other person thinks it is time to buy because the stock will earn a good profit eventually (or quickly) and it will cost him more if he waits to buy it later on, or it may offer good steady dividends. Sometimes motives can be more complicated, of course. People also sell because they need the cash, even when a stock still looks promising.

What the buyer and seller have in common is that each is looking to the future. Each tries to guess what is going to happen to the market and to specific investments in the days, months, or years to come. And each hopes to make some money—or at least protect the value of his assets—on the strength of his guesses.

Nobody can predict market movements for sure. Still, there are many investing techniques that can help you and your wife build for the future with reasonable assurance. These are concepts you can and should teach your wife. She can help you plan for the future now, as well as learn to protect her own interests if you should die.

Secure your family's welfare first

Before you start investing, remember this caution: Don't get involved with investments until you have adequate savings and insurance programs. Even the soundest-appearing investments can go awry, so a family's welfare should be secure before one seeks greater returns through investments.

Why invest at all? One good reason is inflation. Remember that a problem with insurance, discussed earlier, was the probable loss of purchasing power of the dollar over the years. Yet, it has been demonstrated that money invested in 1935 in common stocks overall (individual stocks may have faltered) has kept pace with inflation. The value of stocks has increased at least as much as, and in many cases more than, the cost of living.

Stock Market Ups and Downs

**Major swings in two decades as measured
by the Dow Jones Industrial Average**

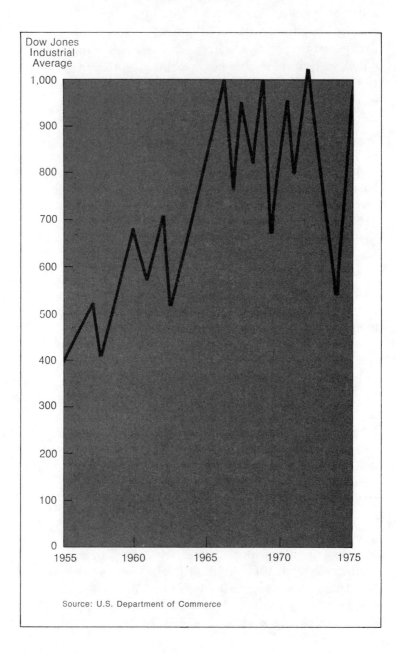

Source: U.S. Department of Commerce

Any well-run family budget will include plans for an investment program, either for the present or the future.

If you have planned wisely, your widow will inherit some stocks when you die. But even if you haven't, she will probably inherit a substantial sum of cash.from your insurance and from other benefits you have acquired along the way. A man who earns $15,000 a year will generally leave an insurance policy larger than that. So will a man who earns $50,000. And so on.

What will your widow do with this cash?

Will she realize that even though she may feel "rich" at first, there will be no further income unless she earns it herself or her money earns it for her? Will she rush out to buy that expensive fur coat she has always wanted? Or will she be thoroughly indoctrinated in the cautious procedure she should follow? Will she put aside enough for current expenses, pay up your bills and funeral expenses, and then take a good portion of the remainder to a trusted broker?

And once she has invested her money and is realizing some income from it, will she know how to trade on the securities exchanges? Will she know when to buy more stock, or when to sell the stock she holds, so that she can make her investment grow and prosper?

It doesn't take a formal education to be a clever investor. The "education" costs a few pennies a day —basically in the daily newspapers, financial publications, and magazines. Your wife can be involved with your own investing right now. These are the things she should know: of primary importance is the political and economic health of the nation; of secondary importance is the stability of a corpora-

tion and the efficiency, progressiveness, and fore-
sightedness of the corporation management; of
least importance is what traders are doing with
stock at any particular moment on Wall Street.

A famous economist once said the best way to
make money in the stock market is to buy stock
when it's low and sell it when it's high. He wasn't
being facetious. You have to know when to buy, but
that's only half the trick; you have to know when
to sell.

Your wife's interest in the business-economic-
financial news of the world will grow as she relates
it to her own welfare and security. A tax bill being
argued in Congress can mean more than extra income tax she will have to pay. The bill also may
require more taxes to be levied on some industries,
and thus could affect their profit potential. She will
find significance in such formerly dull statistical
information as retail sales, carloadings, steel production, electric production, food consumption, the
price of cotton, and the price of hogs.

If she owns two shares of a department store's
stock, she will be concerned not only about retail
sales but also about the rate of personal income, the
amount of savings in banks, the prospect of higher
freight rates, whether wool prices might fall (leaving the store with a costly inventory of suits which
can't compete with suits made of cheaper wool),
and rumors of new wage increases for sales personnel.

One way to enlighten her is to let her decide, on
the basis of study of available financial information, what stock she would like to buy. Let's say she
chooses a utility company which is running a new
natural gas pipeline into an area of the country.
Let her pretend to "invest" a few dollars in the se-

lected utility stock and keep careful check on the movement of the stock on the market. It may take months to know if her choice has been wise, but she will learn by trial and error without risking a cent.

Before she starts investing, it is wise to review with her some of the fundamental principles and terms of the market. Your wife may be familiar with many stock market terms, but still it will be helpful to clarify her thinking.

An important first step is for your wife to decide why she wants to invest. What does she want her investments to accomplish? She might be interested in steady income, through dividends paid out of the company's earnings, or through interest, through loan-type securities. Or she may be looking for her best profit from "capital gains"—one of the key concepts in investment. A capital gain is the profit made when selling certain kinds of property, such as stocks or real estate. If such property is held for over six months before selling it, the profit or loss becomes a "long-term" capital gain or loss. There can be some significant tax advantages when capital gains are long term, as will be seen in the following chapter.

Investment goals

Explain that some securities are basically *income-producing*. Under this classification would come bonds, for instance, or some of the high-priced "blue chip" stocks of well-established companies such as General Motors Corporation. Other securities promise *growth*. Often these are newer companies, or companies in expanding industries. Typically, these corporations do not pay spectacular dividends, and some pay none at all. They prefer to reinvest earnings in the company, thus encourag-

Land vs. Stocks: The Investment Record

(1960=100)

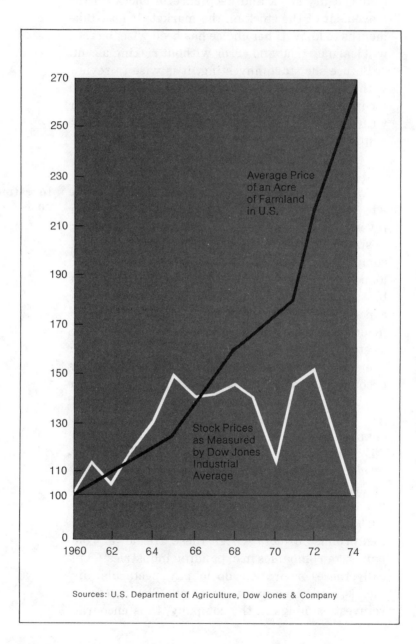

Average Price
of an Acre
of Farmland
in U.S.

Stock Prices
as Measured
by Dow Jones
Industrial
Average

Sources: U.S. Department of Agriculture, Dow Jones & Company

ing capital growth over the years. The result of this policy is that the value of the stock itself is likely to go up considerably over the long run. A third type of stock is the relatively conservative one that offers a reasonable rate of return in dividends, as well as modest appreciation in value.

Usually, younger people concentrate on growth stocks, hoping to build their assets over the years. In their middle years, they probably want some growth as well as some income-producing securities. And in their later years, income most likely is their primary interest.

Your widow's goal probably would be to receive a steady income from investments without depleting capital. Many brokers recommend a balanced portfolio with emphasis on "defensive" securities. This Wall Street term means the securities are usually unassailable by fluctuations in the economy and are designed to protect capital and to maintain regular dividend income. Such companies would be leaders in their respective industrial fields and characterized by strong financial positions, good earnings, and records of unbroken dividend payments over a long period of years.

A widow will want to look for dividend rates that appear well protected by corporate earnings, so that her annual return seems secure. The market action of her portfolio should show above-average stability. Despite occasional fluctuation in some of the stocks, the portfolio should be such that the market prices are unlikely to fall severely over the long haul, and such that she is unlikely to lose any significant capital.

She should not have to pump additional money into her portfolio to maintain an even income. Should she need to sell some of her stock to raise money in an emergency, she should not be forced to take a severe capital loss because the value of the stock has declined. On the contrary, there should be the prospect that some of these stocks will increase in value, though none of them, in any respect, should be what are considered "speculative" issues —that is, those that might plunge ahead to new highs (or drop drastically to new lows).

This is not to say that there should not be several "growth" stocks in your widow's portfolio. For reasons of inflation alone, it is essential that her capital grow to some extent. But remember—the greater the chance for growth, the greater the risk usually. Even her choices of growth stocks should be on the conservative side.

. Such advice from stockbrokers may be all well and good, but how does she really know what she is doing? How does she put together and maintain a portfolio of investments that will meet her goals? Probably the portfolio should include some mixture of different kinds of securities, so it is important for her to know the various types and what they can do for her.

Two types of securities   Explain to your wife that there are two major types of securities—stocks and bonds—and they have two very different functions.

Stocks:

When she buys *stocks* she literally buys "a share in American industry." She becomes a part-owner of the company, and thus holds a claim to a proportionate share in everything from profits and losses to—ultimately—machinery, buildings, even typewriter ribbons.

As a stockholder, she receives a share of the com-

pany's profits in the form of dividends. Usually,
these are paid each business quarter, but sometimes a company will not declare a dividend at all.
What she earns or does not earn depends upon the
fortunes of the business. As profits increase, her
earnings are likely to increase as well—directly,
through larger dividends, or indirectly, through ex-
pansion of the company's assets as its directors
reinvest the retained earnings back into the operation. If she sells her stock, she is likely to have a
capital gain, too. That is, the market value of her
stock will have risen, since other investors will have
perceived the value of "her" company's stock and,
true to the law of supply and demand, driven its
price up in their competition to own some shares.

Conversely, if profits drop or business looks bad
for other reasons, her income through dividends
most likely will drop as well. If she sells her stock
at this point, she also could suffer a capital loss as
investors flee the bad situation by selling, thus
causing the price to drop below that at which she
purchased the stock.

She should know that the purpose of issuing a
stock is to raise money for the company. She may
hear about a stock's *par value* or its *book value,* but
these terms have nothing to do with the current
value of the stock. *Market value* is the crucial, vis-
ible measure of what a security is worth currently.
Market prices are quoted in whole, halves, quarters,
or one-eighths of a dollar. Thus, a stock at 19⅛
would be selling at $19.12½ per share. One at 37¾
would be worth $37.75. The market price is, quite
simply, what people are willing to pay for a share
in the company at a given time. Generally, this
judgment focuses on the company's earnings—current and projected. Other factors include what's

happening to sales, costs, and taxes, as well as the general economic climate and mood of the market.

In owning stocks she will participate in the ups and downs of the company's profits and losses, according to the type of stock she owns. *Common stocks* generally offer her the chance for the greatest gains or losses. In a good year, dividends and market value may rise significantly; in a bad year, the reverse can happen. *Preferred stocks* provide her with greater security, but do not share in company or industry growth or market rises to the extent that common stocks do. Usually, preferred dividends must be paid before dividends on the commons are distributed. That is one reason their prices are more stable. With some preferreds— called "cumulatives"—dividends that were not paid during any year become cumulative and must be paid at a future date before dividends may be paid on regular preferreds or common stock. If the corporation dissolves, preferred shareholders come before common shareholders when the company's assets are distributed.

Often, preferred shares sell for more on the market than common shares and, as already said, their prices do not fluctuate to the same degree. However, *convertible preferreds* have more latitude, because they can be exchanged by the owner at any time for common stock of the same company at a preestablished ratio. Their value is more likely to go up and down significantly in relation to the fortunes or ills of the common stock to which they may be converted.

Most preferred issues also have a redemption provision, which allows the company the right to call, or redeem, the issue. In other words, they buy it back at a preestablished price.

Because of the more stable dividend procedures, preferred stocks can be a good steady-income investment. Often that's exactly what a widow wants —extra cash coming in on a regular basis with minimal danger of eroding capital assets. Redemption and conversion possibilities should be weighed carefully, however. She wants to be sure that the current price of the stock is not a great deal higher than what its redemption price would be. Nor does she want to lose money unnecessarily because the prearranged ratio of preferred-to-common is unfavorable at the time she would want to exchange her convertible shares. This usually takes some expert figuring with a competent broker.

Bonds:

Your widow's least risky form of securities investing can be through bonds. Tell her that, unlike stocks, which provide actual shares of ownership in a company, bonds are loans that are made to the company. At an established time, the date of *maturity,* she is assured the return of the bond's stated value when it was issued. Whether she gains or loses on that amount depends upon what she paid when she bought the bond. In the meantime, she receives annual interest on her loan at a specified rate.

Explain that there are three major varieties of bonds: those issued by the federal government (see Chapter 7); those issued by corporations; and those issued by local governments ("municipals"). Tell her that, with the exception of some government issues, most bonds are sold in $1,000 denominations. Thus a twenty-year, $1,000 bond for the XYZ Company at 7 percent interest will pay her $70 a year for twenty years—a total of $1,400— and she will get back the original $1,000 at that time. (Actually, she may have paid less than $1,000 when she bought the bond, as she will learn later.) If she were to put her widow's inheritance of, say, $20,000 into the same XYZ twenty-year bonds, she would receive $1,400 a year, or $116.66 a month income, a total of $28,000 over twenty years; and her original investment would remain intact for her or her heirs twenty years from the time she bought the bonds.

Your wife may have heard the description of the rich widow who "just sits at home clipping coupons." She should know that the reference is to a *coupon bond*. Each time interest is due, the bond owner detaches and cashes a coupon that is attached to the certificate. Usually, coupon bonds are issued only to the *bearer*, and the company has no record of the owner. This can cause problems. For one thing, bearer bonds are freely negotiable pieces of paper and should be guarded carefully, probably in a safe deposit box. For another, bondholders sometimes forget, or are not aware of, the date the bonds are to be redeemed. The company must advertise the redemption date, but if it goes unnoticed by the bondholder and enough time passes—ten years, for example—the redemption sum may actually be paid over to the state through a legal process called "escheat." State laws vary on how, when, and if this can happen.

Also tell your wife about *registered bonds,* which automatically carry the name of the owner. Interest and principal are paid by check—and only to the owner who is named on the bond.

Inform your wife that in a corporation, bondholders take precedence over preferred and common stock shareholders. Assuming the company does not go bankrupt, she is reasonably assured of receiving her interest and principal according to the contract her bond purchase represents. Bonds are given financial and quality ratings according to certain standards set by Moody's *Bond Record* and Standard & Poor's *Bond Guide,* and her broker can tell her about any bond's quality. Ratings run from AAA down to D. She should feel reasonably secure with any bond in the A range.

Your wife should be told that the main problem with bonds has been inflation, although in recent years bonds have become especially attractive because many have yielded a 7 or 8 percent return while many common stocks have yielded only 3 or 4 percent. With bonds, she knows there will be a regular, predictable income for her each year and that the original investment will remain intact and be available at a predetermined time. However, she must consider how inflation affects that situation: a twenty-year bond bought in 1949 for $1,000 had the purchasing power of only $560 of its original worth at maturity because the value of the dollar had declined so much. Also, let's say that the bond paid $57.50 each year at a $5\frac{3}{4}$ percent rate. That sum was worth only about $35 twenty years later.

Bonds produce regular income

For an older widow whose projected life span might be only another few years, the guaranteed income from bonds could be essential. The inflationary factor would not be too important over the short term and the fixed income might be more important than preserving the capital in constant dollars for her heirs. Looked at that way, 7 percent bonds (fairly typical these days) provide a decent assured income if she owns enough of them.

Tell your wife that, although bonds are sold in

How Bonds Are Rated

Standard & Poor's	Moody's	
AAA	Aaa	The best; least risk.
AA	Aa	High grade; minimal risk.
A	A A-1	Medium grade; little risk. (Moody's A-1 indicates best bonds in this group.)
BBB	Baa Baa-1	Less reliable. (Moody's Baa-1 indicates best bonds in this group.)
BB	Ba	Slightly more speculative.
B	B	Lack desirable characteristics.
CCC	Caa	Lower quality; highly speculative.
CC	Ca	
C	C	
Nonrated		Standard & Poor's and Moody's do not usually rate bonds of communities with under $600,000 debt, and Moody's also does not always rate revenue projects under construction.

denominations of $1,000 (their *par value*), the actual price may be higher or lower than that on the market. That's why prices are quoted as a percentage of par value. For example, point out to her that a price of 83 means the $1,000 bond currently is selling for $830. One of the risks of bonds is that if she has to sell before the maturity date, the price may have dropped, and she could lose part of her investment.

Be sure she understands that a key to trading in bonds is the fact that when general interest rates in the business community go up, bond prices go down; and when interest rates go down, bond prices go up. She can be shown the reasons in terms of the law of supply and demand: When money is hard to get, interest rates are high. New bonds will offer higher rates of return to attract buyers, and anyone holding older bonds at lower rates will want to sell and get in on the higher promised return. That means price competition, for if you offer to sell at a bit less than the next person, you are likely to close the deal. As people realize that fact, the prices slide rapidly.

By the same token, if interest rates are down and new bond issues reflect this situation, the bond you already own becomes more valuable because it pays more than the new issues. In view of the greater value of the bond you own, more people want it, and competition drives the price upward.

These rules of the marketplace often make it possible to find real bargains. If she can spot some highly rated bonds selling considerably below par value—say, in a range of 60 to 80, which is $400 to $200 below the $1,000 maturity redemption figure —she has two promising possibilities:

First, she will realize a significant capital gain if

she holds the bond to maturity. Second, the price might go up dramatically in a very short time if interest rates go down even by so little as 1 percent. In this case, her current yield, which is the annual interest divided by the price of the bond, may be low. On a *deep discount* bond selling at, say, 70 with an interest rate of 5½ percent, the current yield is almost 8 percent ($55 annual interest divided by $700 current price). But she will get $1,000 when the bond matures, and that $300 ($1,000 less $700) profit is figured into what brokers call *yield to maturity*. In this case, depending upon when in the bond's lifetime she bought it, the yield to maturity would be considerably more than the current yield of 8 percent.

Brokers have all sorts of tables, called "basis books," to compare such factors instantly in any given situation, and certainly neither you nor your wife should get involved with bond speculation without expert advice. The point both of you should remember is that bonds can provide steady income, if that is what you are looking for; or they can serve as a more speculative medium, if you prefer to trade in them and look for capital gains.

Municipal bonds are in a category by themselves, since you pay no federal (and usually no state) income tax on the interest earned. These bonds are issued by states, counties, and other local authorities to finance public projects, and the tax-exempt factor is designed to encourage the public to participate in such financing. However, that particular tax break has been sharply criticized in recent years (as have the gift tax and estate tax laws), and it is possible some modification of the tax-exempt rules will be passed by Congress.

As you probably know, and should tell your wife,

the particular appeal of tax-exempt municipal
bonds under current law is that the higher the income tax bracket, the more value the bonds offer in
real income. If your net taxable income is between
$32,000 and $36,000, for instance, you are in the 42
percent bracket. At that tax rate, you would have to
find an investment paying 9.48 percent in order to
match the yield of a 5½ percent municipal bond.
This table will give your wife an idea of the real
gain with 5½ percent tax-free bonds in a number
of tax brackets.

Taxable Income Joint Return, After Deductions and Exemptions	Income Tax Bracket	A tax-free bond that yields 5½% is equal to a taxable investment with this yield:
$12,000 to $16,000	25%	7.33%
$16,000 to $20,000	28%	7.64%
$20,000 to $24,000	32%	8.09%
$24,000 to $28,000	36%	8.59%
$28,000 to $32,000	39%	9.02%
$32,000 to $36,000	42%	9.48%
$36,000 to $40,000	45%	10.00%
$40,000 to $44,000	48%	10.58%
$44,000 to $52,000	50%	11.00%
$52,000 to $64,000	53%	11.70%
$64,000 to $76,000	55%	12.22%
$76,000 to $88,000	58%	13.10%
$88,000 to $100,000	60%	13.75%
$100,000 to $120,000	62%	14.47%
$120,000 to $140,000	64%	15.28%
$140,000 to $160,000	66%	16.18%
$160,000 to $180,000	68%	17.19%
$180,000 to $200,000	69%	17.74%
Over $200,000	70%	18.33%

Source: *U.S.News & World Report*

Why stocks fluctuate

Here's how you can explain changes in stock values to your wife: The market exists by virtue of differences of opinion; different people think different things will happen in the future. Overall, prices of stock are determined by how investors evaluate what is going on in the world, the nation's economy, specific industries, and individual companies. Although some people are in the market for pure speculation, jumping from one security to another to take advantage of short-range price fluctuations, most investors are in for the long haul. They look at stocks as a way to stay even with inflation and, hopefully, to beat it.

Security analysts are professionals who do just what their name implies: they analyze securities. They scrutinize general market conditions, probe deeply into industries they believe look promising in the light of world events, and keep close tabs on individual companies within those industries.

You can give as an example an analyst who decides that a special type of computer system will gain in commercial importance. He will look at the past performance of several companies in this industry. He will visit the plants, get to know the company officers, and probably keep in touch with performances over quite a long period before making a decision about what companies look most promising.

Most investors do not have the time or expertise to probe into the stocks they are considering the way security analysts do. However, your wife will benefit from understanding the approach an analyst takes—trying to determine what is happening to the economy in relation to global, national, and local current events; searching for industries that seem likely to benefit from these events; seeking the companies in those industries that appear to be best managed and to hold the strongest promise for the future. She can do some similar research on her own, and she should take advantage of whatever research and expert opinion her broker and his colleagues can offer (some brokers offer more than others). The final decisions should be hers, but it is important to employ all resources available to her.

She can learn from you that one feature a broker looks at carefully is the *price-earnings (P/E) ratio,* or *multiple,* of a stock. Explain that this is the current market price of the stock, divided by the latest annual earnings. (Actual dividends paid to shareholders usually are just a portion of these earnings.) A stock priced at 30 that earned $2 per share over the last twelve months has a P/E ratio of 15. One priced at 70 earning $5 has a P/E of 14. And one at 17½ earning $1.75 has a P/E of 10. Tell her that these multiples are subject to fluctuation, depending upon market conditions, public evaluation of the stock's earning potential, and other factors, but usually the ratio swings within fairly definite limits. (A broker can help her determine the significance of where the ratio stands in terms of a company's general performance and the current market.)

Explaining the price-earnings ratio

She will understand that analysts study the P/E factors and, taking market and world conditions into account, as well as facts about the specific company, decide whether a stock is currently undervalued, overvalued, or just about right in terms of its earnings. If in their estimation a stock is undervalued, the time might be favorable for buying, provided there are no indications that the market itself

may be headed for a serious and lengthy price slide
(a *"bear market"*). If an upward-moving *"bull
market"* is in the offing, buying that undervalued
security will prove to be a bargain, since its price
is likely to rise with the rest of the market. On the
other hand, when analysts conclude that a stock
has become overvalued, they will recommend a sell.

**How
she can
follow
stocks**   Your wife may not have direct access to company
managements the way security analysts do, but an
abundance of information nevertheless is available
to her. Certainly, general news always is pertinent
as she tries to anticipate how the market will be
affected by current and future events. In fact, current events have such impact that the market has
had to close on certain occasions to prevent an un-
healthy rash of selling. This occurred when Presi-
dent John F. Kennedy was assassinated, for instance; the New York Stock Exchange suspended
trading to avoid possible panic. (There are other
safeguard mechanisms to control the movement of
the market itself. One example is the power of the
Federal Reserve Board to change the *margin limit*
—the amount that can be bought on credit—if the
market seems to be moving upward too quickly and
unrealistically.)

She can learn about investing in general from the
people in the business. The New York Stock Exchange (11 Wall Street, New York, New York
10005) and the American Stock Exchange (86
Trinity Place, New York, New York 10006) will
provide her with general literature about investing. So will the National Association of Security
Dealers, Over-the-Counter Information Bureau
(120 Broadway, New York, New York 10005), which

oversees the "over-the-counter" market. This market, in brokerage parlance called *OTC*, is the nationwide network of dealings in securities that for the most part are not listed on the two major exchanges or on the several regional exchanges that are scattered throughout the country. Incidentally, any time she is in New York, a visit to both stock exchanges can be very educational. Each has tours designed to explain investing procedures and how the exchanges work.

Most brokers' offices provide literature as well as periodic reports on various companies and industries. Usually, they will send basic literature if she asks for it, but to gain access to their libraries she may have to be a client or a potential one. It is true, as has been reported in the press, that some brokers do not wish to handle small accounts—say, under $25,000. However, many welcome them. If she has trouble on this score, she should write the New York Stock Exchange for its list of some 300 brokers who have stated their readiness to accept small orders.

It's a good idea for her to understand some of the broker's problems with small accounts. Explain that all stock trades involve a commission (of about 2 percent of the total dollar value of the order) to the broker for his time and paperwork. An order of any kind costs the broker somewhere between $32 and $46 to handle the paperwork; the median cost is about $40. This is the case for even the largest firms and whatever the size of the order. The problem arises from the fact that there is not much return on small orders. Generally, stocks are bought and sold in *round lots* of 100 shares. Anything less is called an *"odd lot,"* and the commission on such a transaction for, say $500, would be around 3 percent, or $15. In addition to the commission, she would pay an "odd lot differential" of a few cents per share.

Her broker will have a number of useful reference books on hand such as Standard & Poor's *Stock Reports,* which regularly publishes up-to-date summaries of almost 5,000 companies, and *Moody's Handbook of Common Stocks.* In addition, she can get annual reports from specific companies, as well as some of the Standard & Poor's guides from her broker. And there are a number of sophisticated and often helpful investment services, costing anywhere from $10 to $250 a year. The financial pages of newspapers and magazines can also be useful.

If she has a substantial sum of money to invest, she may wish to consult an investment counselor, who will manage her investments for a fee—typically, 2 percent of her total assets. (She will also pay the brokerage fees.) These experts, with some exceptions, usually refuse accounts smaller than $100,000. Her bank also may offer investment help for a nominal fee.

Probably her best person-to-person guide will be her stockbroker. It is important that she establish a good working relationship with him. He should be fully cognizant of her financial situation, know how much she can safely put into the market, and understand her particular goals. She will pay a commission on each transaction, so she should be sure to avoid a broker who for his own gain will "churn" her account, suggesting that she buy and sell frequently. Her investment should be made with her future security in mind, not for quick profit, and certainly not to benefit the broker by building large commissions for his pocket.

She can follow the market on her own, too. Most

major newspapers publish daily information about New York Stock Exchange and American Stock Exchange transactions, including information about insurance and bank stocks, over-the-counter trades, and mutual funds. Reading these reports regularly is an excellent way to gain a sense of the market and its workings. She should read the financial news items in the same section. Before long, she will have a sense of trends and cause-and-effect patterns.

The following reproductions from the *New York Times*, January 25, 1973, of reports of market activity on the preceding day will give her an idea of how to read the market reports:

New York Stock Exchange:

1972-73 High	Low	Stocks and Div. In Dollars	Sls. 100s	P/E	High	Low	Last	Net Chng
35⅜	18⅛	Matsush .28e	362	12	30⅜	29¼	29½	—1
.....	.....	Matsu fn.28e	13	...	28⅞	27½	27½	....
34¾	10	Mattel .10	458	...	11	10¼	10¼	— ½
54⅞	38¾	MayDStr 1.60	49	15	46⅜	46	46	+ ¼
32⅜	25	MayerOsc .65	11	18	31¾	31½	31¾	+ ⅛
26¾	11	MaysJW .50	43	8	11¾	11½	11⅛	— ⅜
46¼	33	Maytag 1.20a	59	18	38¾	37	37	—1¾
35⅞	23⅛	MCA inc .64	12	12	29½	28½	28½	—1⅛
29⅜	20	McCord .88	31	9	21½	20½	20½	— ¾
32½	21	McCrory 1.20	289	6	27¾	25⅜	25⅜	—2⅛
80¼	32¼	McDermott 1	140	37	78	77	77¼	—1⅛
77⅜	50	McDonalds	273	81	73⅞	71⅜	72¾	— ¾
46⅞	32½	McDonD .40b	162	10	33⅞	33⅜	33¾	+ ⅛
45	33⅞	McG Ed 1.50	47	15	37⅞	37	37⅞	+ ⅛
20⅞	13¼	McGrwH .48	279	18	15⅞	14⅞	14¾	— ⅛
34½	25	Mc GH .pf1.20	21	...	26	25¾	25¾	—1
8⅛	4⅛	McGreg Don	18	20	4½	4⅜	4⅜	+ ⅛
95	41½	McIntyre	z210	...	50⅜	49	49	—2¼
20⅜	15⅜	McKee .45e	6	9	18¾	18½	18½	.....
47	28½	McLeanT .60	35	13	44¾	43¾	44¾	+1¼
24	15⅛	McLouth Stl	47	31	19½	18¾	18¾	— ¼
20¼	12¾	McNeil .70	12	8	13¾	13½	13½	.....
21¼	13⅜	Mead Cp .60	903	15	16½	15½	15¾	— ¼
46½	39½	Mead pfA2.80	2	...	42	41½	41½	.....
47	40	Mead pfB2.80	4	...	41	41	41	.....

Over-the-Counter Market:

	Sls in 100s	Bid	Asked	Bid Chg.
Park Ohio .15e	13	10¼	10¾	...
Parker Drilling	111	34½	34¾	— ⅝
Parkview Gem	12	3¼	3¾	....
Patrick Petrol	176	9½	9⅞	....
Paul Rev I 1.15e	18	17⅜	17⅞	— ⅛
Pauley Petrolm	45	5⅞	6¼	...
Pavella Corp	183	1⅞	2⅛	—1⅛
Pay Less Drg .30	9	14⅞	15⅜	— ⅛
Pay n Pak .15e	59	19⅜	20⅛	— ⅞
Pay n Save .18	38	17	17½	— ¾
Payless Cash .20	39	28	29	—1¼
Paysaver Catalg	11	4⅞	5⅜	— ⅛
Peachtre Dr .06e	28	16	16½	— ¾
Pelto Oil	105	23½	24	—1½
Penn Corp	11	12½	13	— ¼
Penn Gs Wt 1.35	31	19¾	20¼	— ¼
Pennz Offs Gs B	699	8½	8¾	+ ⅛
Pentair Indust	31	6½	6⅞	...
Petersn H&H .27	34	35¼	36	— ¾
Petro Lewis	100	14¾	14¾	—1¼
Phoenix Candy	11	5¼	6	....

The left section is from the New York Stock Exchange. It shows:

1. *1972-73 High-Low*. These are the highest and lowest prices paid for the stock during the year, from the beginning of 1972 to January 24, 1973.

2. *Stocks and Dividends in Dollars*. Here she will find the company's name, often with its own special abbreviation. The letters "pf" mean preferred stock. The figure that follows shows the amount of annual disbursements over twelve months based on the last quarterly or semiannual declaration by the company. The letter "e" means the amount paid in the preceding twelve months. An "xd" would mean the corporation has just declared a dividend but the time for purchasing the stock in order to get the dividend has passed. The letter "a" means that there is also an extra dividend, or even more than one. All these and other such letters are explained in a special note carried on the market pages each day.

3. *Sales in Hundreds*. That's the number of round lots traded on the given day. Odd lots are not shown on the table.

4. *P/E* means price-earnings ratio, and this is a relatively new listing provided by the *New York Times* and the *Wall Street Journal*. Not all papers carry it. Its meaning was explained earlier in this chapter.

5. *High*. The highest price paid for the stock that day.

6. *Low*. The lowest price paid that day.

7. *Last*. The stock's price in the final transaction of the day.

8. *Net Change*. How much a share went up or down that day, compared to the closing price of the day before.

In other words, on January 24, 1973, this was the position of McGraw Edison ("McG Ed"), the huge utilities company: Its high for the past year was $45; its low, $33.37½. Dividends totaled $1.50 per share over the past four quarters. That day saw 4,700 shares sold. Since the price-earnings ratio was 15, total annual earnings were about $2.50 per share (37⅜ divided by 15, approximately). Remember, earnings are not the same thing as dividends; usually a company retains some earnings and pays out the rest in dividends. High sale for the day was $37.87½ per share; its low, $37.00; and it closed at $37.37½ per share. That represented a rise of 12½ cents per share from the day before.

The other section of the chart gives information about some securities traded over-the-counter that day. Notice that there is no listing in terms of high and low of the day. That's because figures were not yet available. Instead, the information given concerns bid and asked prices. Actual sales, when they took place, ranged somewhere between those extremes.

Over-the-counter listings

1. First, there is the company name, or its abbreviation.

2. Second, you see dividend information.

3. *Sales in Hundreds* is shown the same way as with the New York Stock Exchange.

4. *Bid* shows the price securities dealers were willing to pay for the stock.

5. *Asked* shows what dealers were willing to sell it for.

6. *Bid Change* shows the difference between the bid price on January 24 and the bid price at the end of the day before. If there is no figure given, there

was no change in the bid from the previous day.

Other Wall Street terms that may be useful for her to know:

Cash Sales. This term has to do with the delivery date of stocks. When shares are bought in the conventional manner, the selling broker must deliver them to the buying broker no later than the fifth full business day following the sale. Should the buying broker want immediate delivery, he would buy for cash. The selling broker would be making a "cash sale." Such sales are very prevalent at year's end when time is short and cash sales may bring gains or losses desired before the new income tax year, which begins January 1.

Market Averages. These are averages of the market prices of a selected number of stocks in selected industry groups. They are used to keep a record of progress of the stock market and the general tone of the financial community. The Dow Jones and Standard & Poor's averages are widely known and cited in newspapers and magazines.

Street Names. Not all stock certificates are held by their owners. Sometimes buyers of shares prefer to have them held by their brokers. Thus, when dividends are declared, the check is not sent to the rightful owner, but to the broker or to a "Street Name," who credits the money to the owner's account. One advantage of owning in a "Street Name" is that transactions are not delayed by an owner's having to locate certificates of shares he is selling and send them to his broker. The broker already has them. This is advantageous if an investor is traveling, for instance, and unable to reach his safe deposit box.

Puts and Calls. These are methods of obtaining options to buy or sell stock (seldom less than 100 shares at a time) within a specified period of time. With a "put" or "call" option, you risk only a fraction of the actual cost of the securities, and you make a profit if the stock moves a few points or more in the right direction during your time limit. The whole procedure takes sophisticated know-how and is not recommended for an individual living on a relatively fixed income who cannot afford to lose capital.

Commodities Futures. Although a valid form of investing, this market has nothing to do with securities as discussed in this chapter. Nor is it for anyone who cannot afford to lose $5,000 or $10,000 or much more. (Gains can be equally spectacular, of course.) The commodities market provides a way to bet on the future market price of commodities such as grain, hog bellies, silver, and so on. It is a very fast-moving procedure and one you probably should stay away from unless you have the time, courage, and disposable cash to become an expert.

Greater gains, less risk

Your wife has already seen how bonds and preferred stocks can provide a reasonably assured return, but often without the appreciation required to keep ahead of inflation or build capital significantly. Common stocks offer the greatest possibility of capital growth, but with great risk, too. What can she do to benefit from the long-range growth of the economy without placing her assets in jeopardy?

One way could be through *dollar cost averaging.* This is an investment program in which she puts a specific amount at regular intervals into one or more stocks that she has chosen. If the market drops, she is buying more shares with her money;

if the market rises, she is buying fewer shares. In the long run, she should make money this way—presuming the market has risen overall, and her stock or stocks have risen with it.

Let's say she decides to put $100 a month into XYZ Company's common stock. She buys initially at 30, which means her $100 will buy about 3⅓ shares. Next month, the price drops to 28; her $100 buys 3.6 shares. Next month, 25; 4 shares. Next, 27: 3.7 shares. Then 32: 3.1 shares. Finally, in the sixth month, the price rises to 36, which buys her 2.8 shares.

Her total purchase over the six months is 20.5 shares of XYZ common stock. Her total investment has been $600. The average price per share was about $29.25 ($600 divided by 20.5). But her 20.5 shares are now worth $36 each, or a total of $738. That's a $138 profit, or almost a 23 percent return on her money—excluding some minor commission costs, of course.

To use this method of investment, she must maintain a fairly rigid discipline. Once she picks the stock or stocks, she should stay with them even though the price may drop. She should give her program a test of at least a year. Also, she should hold the investment at the same amount of money at regular intervals. It does not matter if she skips a contribution once in a while, but she should make that omission rare. For a more formalized plan of dollar cost averaging, she should ask her broker about the *Monthly Investment Plan* of the New York Stock Exchange.

An *investment club* could also be a fairly safe way for her to invest in the market, although her capital growth won't be spectacular unless she joins a club that requires a sizable contribution each month. Then, of course, she will be risking more cash. Your wife should know that, in essence, investment clubs are organizations with ten or fifteen people who pool some of their money regularly to invest. Typical contributions are $20 to $25 a month. The members meet regularly to talk over the market and specific investment possibilities, and make decisions on buying and selling. All members are required periodically to research specific companies, report to the club, and make recommendations.

Over 10,000 such clubs are operating throughout the country, and their members invest over $2\frac{1}{2}$ million new dollars every month. Although not all have been successful, an impressive number of clubs have kept up with, and even surpassed, the Dow Jones average. Nearly a million members of investment clubs in the United States today speaks well for the plan, too.

Main advantages: She won't risk much money unless she joins a high-capital group; she will learn quite a bit about the market; she will share research and thinking with a number of other concerned people; and she will probably have an enjoyable time. It could be a good pastime for a widow, as well as a profitable, if not spectacular, venture. Probably the club she joins should be affiliated with the National Association of Investment Clubs. For more information, she can write to this organization at: 1515 East Eleven Mile Road, Royal Oak, Michigan 48067.

Mutual funds

Mutual funds have made a strong appeal to the widow who is not inclined to do much homework on her own. However, she still has to select the right fund. Just as some stocks offer growth, others income, and others a balance of the two, so mutual funds are designed to meet specific needs. She will also want to study the management and past performance of several funds before choosing. Funds focusing on income are often recommended to widows. Remember, however, that *there is no guarantee* that successful past performance of a fund will be continued into the future.

You might explain to your wife that, in its simplest form, a mutual fund works this way: The money she, and presumably thousands of others, sends each month is invested in one huge portfolio of securities. The earnings from the portfolio are divided among the mutual fund owners according to the size of the individual's interest, or investment, in the fund.

Easy way to become an investor

There probably is no easier way to become an investor and share in the profits accruing from America's industrial growth. For as little as $50 a month (and sometimes less) invested in a mutual fund, she can become the joint owner of the shares of many thriving corporations. She will minimize her risk if she chooses her fund carefully to begin with, for most funds are invested and managed by experts who are cognizant of each waver and fluctuation in the nation's economy.

Many funds performed spectacularly during much of the 1960s, only to falter severely toward the end of the decade. One problem was that many investors were attracted to the "get-rich-quick" publicity of some of the more volatile funds. However, other funds defended themselves successfully during the recession in the late sixties. It is important that your wife see mutual funds as a long-term investment rather than as a quick road to riches.

According to the Investment Company Institute, which represents the mutual fund industry, $10,000 invested in 1960 and left in until 1969 would have produced $14,581 from Series E government bonds, $15,234 from savings accounts, $16,448 from stocks which kept pace with the Dow Jones average, $21,-255 from an average of all mutual funds (dividends and capital gains reinvested) and $25,458 from successful growth stock funds.

Your wife can choose between a *load* fund, which makes a one-time purchase charge of about 8 percent, and a *no-load* fund, which makes no such charge, so that all her money is working for her right from the start. Good records have been achieved by both the loads and the no-loads.

Brokers sell load funds (thereby requiring a sales commission) but not the no-loads, which are secured directly from the fund concerned. No-loads are listed in a number of reference guides.

For general information about mutual funds, your wife can write: The Investment Company Institute, 1775 K St., N.W., Washington, D.C. 20006; and The No-Load Mutual Fund Association, 475 Park Avenue South, New York, New York 10016. She can also look into *Investment Companies*, published by Weisenberger Services, and *Fundscope*, a periodical specializing in mutual funds. *Forbes* magazine devotes one issue a year to a comparison of fund performances.

9

Death
and
Taxes

Taxes and the ability to cope with them can make a difference between living comfortably and living under extremely disagreeable pressures. This is all the more true in the case of a widow who had left the unpleasant matters of taxes largely in the hands of her husband. As a widow, she no longer has his protection and she is more vulnerable than ever to the income tax collector.

If your wife is to be prepared to deal with the Internal Revenue Service, you must begin at once to inform her about all the details involved in preparing your annual income tax return, and you should train her so that she eventually will be able to handle the return herself. This chapter deals with various aspects of the annual income tax. The next chapter takes up other important taxes affecting your widow's welfare—estate, inheritance, and gift taxes.

The starting point for your wife's education in tax matters should be working with you—learning what sources you use to accumulate your tax material and understanding the information you give your tax adviser.

Your wife will recognize that since such a substantial portion of your income is allocated to taxes, it makes good sense to give the proper time and attention to preparing your return. This means that you must create good records, review them intelligently, and plan for the preparation of your tax returns as soon as possible after the end of the year. Not only will your professional tax adviser be in a better position to give you the necessary attention then, but you are apt to do a more thorough job of putting the information together if you start early and do not have to work under the pressure of time to complete this task.

Individual income tax returns are almost always due April 15 for the preceding year. It is essential that the return be filed on or before that due date to avoid severe penalties and the possibility of criminal prosecution.

The deadline: April 15

Be sure your wife knows that if she is unable to file her return when it is due, she *must* request an extension for filing *before* the due date to avoid penalty. This can be done by obtaining a copy of an application for automatic extension from the district director of Internal Revenue and sending it as certified mail, return receipt requested, on or before April 15. Her state and possibly her city may have

The Tax Bite Gets Bigger

Taxes have soared from a total in 1944 of $48 billion, or 26 percent of the nation's income, to $423 billion, or 37 percent of national income in 1974.

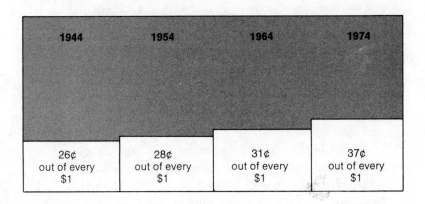

	Federal Taxes		State and Local Taxes	
	Billions	*Percentage of National Income*	*Billions*	*Percentage of National Income*
1944	$ 39.0	21.4%	$ 9.0	4.9%
1954	62.5	20.6	22.2	7.3
1964	111.5	21.5	49.7	9.6
1974	284.7	24.9	138.5	12.1

Source: U.S. Department of Commerce

similar requirements, so she should comply with those as well.

Tell your wife that to figure your taxes, you first determine your *adjusted gross income*. This is the sum of everything you earned during the year from wages, interest, dividends (less a certain amount), any income from a business or profession, taxable pensions and annuities, and so on—all minus any "sick pay," company moving expenses, or other such reimbursements you received during the year. **Figuring income**

Although in theory you pay taxes on all your adjusted gross income, the government reasons that you have the right to some credit for certain expenses and for the number of people you support. These are figured in terms of *deductions* for your expenses and *exemptions* for the dependents.

You have two options about credit for living expenses. You can take a *standard deduction*, which is a fixed amount or percentage that you subtract from your adjusted gross income. Normally the standard deduction is 15 percent of your adjusted gross income up to $2,000. Otherwise, you can *itemize* deductions. This gives you the opportunity to list many items of expense, thus often bringing the total deduction to an amount far larger than allowed with the standard deduction.

Among the expenses eligible for itemizing: interest you pay on loans, sales and property taxes, medical expenses (beyond 3 percent of your adjusted gross income), certain business expenses, and charitable contributions.

You might figure your return both ways so you can take the approach that saves you the greater amount of money.

There is a third option for people with very limited incomes. This is the *low income allowance*, which is normally a flat figure of $1,300 regardless of the amount of income or the number of dependents claimed. The principal effect of this allowance is to eliminate taxes altogether for people with small incomes.

Once you have deducted your expenses from your adjusted gross income, you are allowed to subtract a prescribed amount ($750 usually) called an "exemption" for each person in your family for whom you pay at least half his or her support. That includes you, your wife, your children—even your parents, if you support them and their income does not exceed certain limits. Say your income from various sources is $25,000 and you have three children and a dependent parent. Your dependents' exemptions would bring your taxable income down by $4,500 (six times $750).

After you have subtracted your deductions and exemptions, you pay tax on the balance. That is your *taxable income*. If it is, say, $11,800, you are in the so-called 22 percent tax bracket when you file a joint return. A tax rate of 22 percent applies to all your taxable income between $8,000 and $12,-000. However, your taxable income below $8,000 is taxed in a lower bracket. The formula is provided on the IRS tax charts; you simply calculate in terms of your taxable income figure on that chart.

Keep all records   In order to determine the lowest legal tax, it is essential that records be maintained. What are these records and what is the simplest form of keeping them? With a view toward possible deductions, it is desirable to pay as many bills as possible by check. Preserve *all* canceled checks for a minimum of three years after they are used in filing a tax return. If you purchase a house or stock or make other investments, save the invoices, settlement sheets, broker's confirmations, and other documents for at least three years after you have *disposed* of the investment, stock, or house.

To have an accurate record of all income, it is necessary to maintain a list of all deposits in your checking and savings accounts. It is particularly important that an accurate record be kept when money is borrowed, funds are transferred from one account to another, notes or mortgages are redeemed, or when gifts, inheritances, or similar items are received. A permanent record is the key to avoiding tax complications in the future by being able to identify what went into every bank deposit.

Confirmation and monthly statement notices from stockbrokers should be saved. At the end of every year, you receive notification of the amounts of dividends and interest you have earned. These are called 1099s and they should be maintained as part of your permanent tax records. If you are a member of a partnership or a beneficiary of a trust, you will receive notification of your tax status from them. These forms should also be made part of your permanent tax records available to the individual who is assisting you in the preparation of your returns, as well as available to Internal Revenue in the event you are audited.

If you or your wife inherit any property, stocks, bonds, or real estate, be sure to obtain written guidance from the executors as to the value of the inherited assets for tax purposes. This value is known as your "basis" or "tax basis." If you receive a substantial gift of securities or other valuable property, it is important that you have the donor advise you of your tax basis in that property so that you can measure a gain or loss if you sell it.

Cutting taxes calls for planning   The real planning for tax savings must begin *before* the end of the year. In purchasing investments you and your wife must learn to think in terms of the tax effect of the particular investment. For instance, if you are in a 40 percent tax bracket and you purchase a fully taxable 8 percent bond for $10,000, you will receive $800 a year in taxable interest. Your net income from that bond after federal tax will be $480, or an effective yield of 4.8 percent. On the other hand, if you purchase a $10,000 tax-exempt bond paying 5.5 percent interest, you will have a net yield of $550, or $70 a year more.

Another way in which tax savings can be achieved is by bunching your itemized deductions into years when they will be meaningful rather than indiscriminately claiming them each year. This is known as alternating and can save you tax money.

Also worth planning for are tax-saving capital gains (profits on property or securities held more than six months). Since only half of the gain is subject to tax, a 50 percent reduction can be claimed simply by holding a good investment for a "long term" (at least six months) rather than selling as soon as the market begins to move up. The 50 percent savings in tax can sometimes be worth more than the gain itself.

In the year of bereavement, your widow will be faced with all sorts of psychological and emotional adjustments. Not the least of these will be the problem of grappling with the first tax return that will become due after your death. Hopefully, she will have assisted you in accumulating and preparing the tax returns in previous years and will be familiar with the family's financial affairs. Because of specific legal requirements that court auditors review your estate, it is important to have a careful separation between items belonging to the estate, for which an accounting will have to be made, and those items which belong to your widow and lie outside the estate, thereby not accountable to the government or the courts.

A few examples may be helpful. Let us take the case of Joe and Betty Brown, who have been married many years. Their estate is fairly small, something in the order of $50,000 in securities and the value of their home. Their children are grown. All of their securities and their home are owned jointly. This means that after Joe's death, Betty automatically will own the house and the securities outright without having to file any papers with the court. It may be necessary for her to send a certified copy of the death certificate and stock certificates to the registered agent of the corporation in which she owns securities and ask that they be reissued in her name. In any event, since the assets were owned jointly, they belong to her, and the income earned immediately after her husband's death is her income and is reported on her tax returns thereafter. In the year of her husband's death she will probably elect to file a joint return with her husband. These results would not have been changed if her husband had left a will or if there were minor children.

When assets are owned jointly

The situation is quite different in the case of Harry and Sandy Smith, who similarly owned $50,-000 worth of securities and their home. While their home was owned jointly, the securities were in Harry's name alone. Upon Harry's death, these securities passed to his estate, where they were to be disposed of either in accordance with his will or by the operation of law in the event he did not have a will. Minor children, creditors, and others may have had an interest in the securities Harry had held in his name and, therefore, it was important that dividends received after Harry's death were not included in his final income tax return. The court auditor was looking for those dividends to make certain that they were properly accounted for and deposited in the estate account. The estate had to file its own income tax return.

These illustrations are not intended to imply that joint ownership is desirable in all cases. Rather, they simply point out the importance of understanding what happens to assets owned by the husband and how they are handled on his final tax return.

Your last tax return   The point to bear in mind is that your taxable year ends on the date of your death. Your final income tax return for that part of the year, up to and including the date of death, is filed on the regular form 1040. In most cases, the final tax return is filed as a joint tax return with the widow, and the return is handled by the administrator, executor, or legal representative of the estate. It is due on the normal date for filing individual returns, April 15 in most cases. If no executor or other legal representative is appointed by the court, the widow may file a joint return by signing her deceased husband's name as well as her own name.

Most taxpayers are on what technicians call a cash basis. That means income is reported when it is received and expenses are deductible only when paid.

As an example, consider the case of Dr. and Mrs. James Cole. Dr. Cole was a dentist with $15,000 outstanding in accounts receivable. He died leaving a will which provided for his widow as well as his children. Since the $15,000 in accounts receivable had not yet been collected on the date of his death, they were not included in his final income tax return.

In some states there are laws attempting to simplify the probate of small estates. They offer what is called a "special bond" under which a widow automatically takes the assets. This is usually limited to cases where there are no children, no real estate owned by the deceased in his own name, and where there are enough funds to pay all the creditors. In such cases, the income collected by the widow is automatically hers by "operation of law" and thus included in her return. Competent legal counsel is advisable for handling an estate in this manner.

Your final federal return should always be marked as such, and it should report the date of your death. You are entitled to a full $750 exemption even though you may have lived only one day of your last tax year, and the full standard deduction can be claimed for you. As for state taxes, this is not true in many states where it is necessary to prorate the personal exemption for a deceased individual on a state income tax return. Since this varies from state to state, your widow should check

What Different States Take in Taxes

Amount Collected in Year 1974-75

	Per Person in State's Population	Increase From 1967		Per Person in State's Population	Increase From 1967
Alabama	$284.42	108%	Montana	$299.30	126%
Alaska	$368.43	73%	Nebraska	$262.87	176%
Arizona	$345.19	89%	Nevada	$438.77	123%
Arkansas	$293.61	104%	New Hampshire	$204.41	112%
California	$381.29	110%	New Jersey	$280.53	136%
Colorado	$319.55	88%	New Mexico	$390.08	90%
Connecticut	$353.92	197%	New York	$470.23	113%
Delaware	$537.75	101%	North Carolina	$336.83	101%
Florida	$344.45	136%	North Dakota	$343.32	153%
Georgia	$310.31	110%	Ohio	$259.74	135%
Hawaii	$584.26	97%	Oklahoma	$287.01	79%
Idaho	$320.70	74%	Oregon	$309.63	92%
Illinois	$366.81	176%	Pennsylvania	$389.45	156%
Indiana	$314.11	104%	Rhode Island	$356.09	124%
Iowa	$352.03	114%	South Carolina	$323.83	113%
Kansas	$309.56	98%	South Dakota	$242.85	96%
Kentucky	$329.50	126%	Tennessee	$264.57	100%
Louisiana	$350.56	86%	Texas	$272.86	122%
Maine	$321.25	136%	Utah	$309.54	80%
Maryland	$385.48	121%	Vermont	$382.21	102%
Massachusetts	$380.13	116%	Virginia	$307.22	119%
Michigan	$404.61	127%	Washington	$391.18	56%
Minnesota	$470.55	155%	West Virginia	$340.65	117%
Mississippi	$321.20	145%	Wisconsin	$445.06	102%
Missouri	$272.23	104%	Wyoming	$346.06	97%
U.S. AVERAGE	$352.25	117%			

Source: U.S. Census Bureau

with state tax authorities or competent professional advisers as to how this would apply in her state.

Lump-sum death benefit proceeds from a life insurance policy are not subject to income tax. Also, the first $1,000 of interest earned on death benefit proceeds from a life insurance policy left with an insurance company to be paid out over a period of years is exempt from tax. Social Security and railroad retirement death benefits as well as the regular monthly payments to a widow are not subject to income tax. If your employment arrangement provided a salary continuation plan, the first $5,000 received under such a plan after your death is exempt from tax.

Points to consider

Social Security income can be problematic in terms of whether or not your widow should work, especially if she is young and there are youngsters to support. She should remember that she begins to lose benefits when she earns more than $2,760 in a year. What she makes in salary is taxable beyond certain limits. In terms of the usual limits, your widow could earn up to $2,050 tax-free when she is the only exemption, $2,800 if there is one dependent, $3,550 if there are two other dependents, and so on. This is figured by taking the $1,300 tax-free *low income allowance* alternative to the standard deduction, and adding to it the number of exemptions, at $750, that she will be allowed. She should not forget that she counts as an exemption herself. It all may come down to a decision of whether working is worth giving up the tax-free income from Social Security. Possibly some part-time arrangement would make the most sense, so that she is earning money only during certain months and can collect full Social Security benefits during the other months.

Your wife may benefit from learning about the California widow in her late sixties who unwittingly got into trouble with the tax men because she failed to file a return. Her income came solely from Social Security payments and rather sizable dividends on stocks, and she thought neither was taxable because they did not come from wages or salary. She was right about the Social Security income; she did not have to pay income tax on it. But she was wrong about the dividend income. Even though it was "unearned" and did not count against her Social Security payments, she had to report it to the tax people.

If your employer provided a profit-sharing or pension plan and you had assigned the proceeds to your wife, they are not included in your estate for tax purposes. However, before your widow can determine how much of the amount may be subject to income tax, she will have to contact the trustee of your employer's plan to determine the taxability of the amounts received. Your widow cannot assume that all the money she will receive will be tax-free or subject to tax. It will be necessary that she go to the source and determine the proper tax status in each case.

Special rules may apply to widows of men who receive pensions or annuities from the federal civil service or the armed forces. Similarly, special rules apply to widows who receive pensions by reason of their husband's employment by a nonprofit charitable organization, such as a church, synagogue, or the American Red Cross. In such special cases, the paying authority will usually be available to assist in determining the amount of taxable income that a widow will have as the result of the pension, annuity, or other death benefit paid.

Your widow should always confer with the executors or trustees of your estate before filing her return, either in the year of your death or as long as the estate or any trust created in the estate remains open. The reason for this is that she may be subject to income tax on certain amounts whether distributed to her or not.

Postmortem refund

If you should die early in the year, say January, February, or March, but before filing your return for the preceding year, your widow would be expected to file your return for the year just ended. However, that will not be your final tax return since a final return may be required to include the income for the short period that you lived in the year of death. If you are not required to file a return because of limited earnings in the early months of the year in which you die, it may nevertheless be necessary for your widow to file a return in order to obtain a refund of income withheld from paychecks for taxes. That final return cannot be filed before the end of the calendar year in which you died.

A final income tax return must be filed for a married person who is entitled to file a joint return and who is living in the same household with his wife at the time of his death, if a joint return would show a combined gross income for the year of $2,800 or more ($3,550 if either was 65 or older and $4,300 if both were over 65).

If after computing the final return a refund is due because the tax is less than the amount that was withheld or paid in estimates, a Form 1310, "Statement of Claimant to Refund Due Deceased Taxpayer," must be completed and attached to the income tax return. This form can be obtained from the local district director of Internal Revenue. Most states and the District of Columbia will accept a properly executed copy of Form 1310 for the same purpose.

A special problem arises in connection with medical expenses which are paid from your assets. If these expenses are paid within one year after your death and they are not deducted in computing your taxable estate for federal estate tax purposes, they may be claimed as deductions at the time the expenses were incurred. A careful study will have to be made in consultation with the executors, lawyers, and accountants for the estate to determine where the greatest tax savings lie. Obviously, if you are in the 50 percent tax bracket (taxable income of $44,000 a year or more on a joint return) and your estate is in a lower bracket, it is desirable to claim these expenses on your final income tax return. If your widow elects to deduct these on your final joint return rather than on the estate tax return, she should attach a statement to the income tax return stating that the amount has not been claimed as a deduction on the estate tax return and that it is being waived as a deduction by the estate.

Concessions to widows   Certain special considerations are provided for your widow in the years following the year of your death. One of the most beneficial of these advantages is that she may, under certain circumstances, continue to enjoy the preferred "married filing joint return" rate tables for two years following the year of your death. The special requirements are:

1. She must have been entitled to file a joint return with you in the year of your death (whether or not she actually filed a joint return is immaterial) ;

2. She must not have remarried (if she has remarried, she will of course file a joint return with her new husband) ;

3. She must have a child or a stepchild who qualifies as her dependent;

4. She must furnish over half the cost of maintaining her home, which is the principal residence of her dependent child or stepchild for the entire year except for temporary absences, such as while attending school.

In such cases your widow may file her return for the two years following the year of your death, including only her own income, exemptions, and deductions in computing her taxable income. She should check block five under Filing Status on the front page of Form 1040 and use tax rate schedule "Y" or the column marked "married filing joint return" in the tax tables, which gives her the lower joint return filing rate. She may not claim any exemption or deduction for you in any years after the year of your death.

There are other important considerations. For example, if your widow's taxable income increases in the years after your death, she may use the four preceding years as the basis for "income averaging." This is a special provision which allows an individual whose income increases substantially in any one year to use his average income for the current year and the four preceding years as a basis for computing the tax. Similarly, if your last joint return had either a capital loss carryforward or an operating loss carryforward, your widow may enjoy tax benefits of these carryovers in later years.

Under certain circumstances, she may be entitled to a "deduction for income in respect of a decedent." This relates to an item of gross income that a man would have received had he continued to live. As a result of his death, the money was not included in his final income tax return and, therefore, became subject to estate tax. The following example may help explain this situation.

At the time Harold Johnson died, he was entitled to a large salary payment for deferred commissions. By agreement with his employer, it was to be paid to him in five annual installments. Since he was on a cash basis, the unpaid amounts were included not in his final income tax return but rather in his estate, where it was subject to estate tax. However, the money was not actually collected by Johnson's estate and the right to collect the money was transferred to his widow in accordance with the terms of his will. Nevertheless, the estate paid a federal estate tax on the amount which the widow was later to receive. She, therefore, was entitled to deduct, on her subsequent personal income tax return, the amount of the deferred commissions which had been taken by estate taxes.

Changes in "tax basis"   Another important tax-saving matter a widow should know about is that assets belonging to her husband take a new "tax basis" once she receives them, whether she receives them from the estate or directly by operation of law by reason of her joint ownership of the property, stock, real estate, or other property. Let's see how this works:

Alex and Betty Bowman have been married for thirty years. Except for the first or second year of their marriage, Betty had not worked nor had she received any inheritances or gifts from her family. In the fifteenth year of their marriage, Alex purchased a small apartment house for $36,000. As a matter of convenience, he placed the property in their joint names and collected income on the property throughout all of his remaining years. He claimed depreciation based on his original purchase price. Since the property was owned jointly, it passed to his wife immediately upon his death without going through his estate. Because of inflation and other factors, the value of the property substantially increased and was worth $60,000 at the time of his death. His widow had a new basis for claiming depreciation, which was fixed as the fair market value at the date of death and could start depreciating the property again at the new high value. Further, if she sells the property in later years her "tax basis" for measuring the gain or loss on the sale will be the new tax basis created as a result of her husband's death rather than his original cost. The same would hold true if the property (whether income producing or not, as in the case of their home) first went to his estate and was then distributed to her.

However, the entire property need not have been purchased by the husband, as seen in the following example:

John and Sue Williams were married many years ago. Throughout most of their married life both worked as teachers and earned substantially the same salaries. Their income was deposited in a joint checking account which was later transferred to a savings account. After accumulating a substantial down payment, they bought an apartment house for $36,000, using money in the joint savings account as their down payment. The property was titled in their joint names. When John died, the government recognized the fact that he had purchased only half of the rental property and that Sue owned her half from the time the property was purchased. Therefore, the part she purchased was not included in John's estate and she had to revalue only his portion. Assuming that the property was worth $60,000 at the date of her husband's death, Sue owned two halves of the apartment house each having a separate "tax basis." The portion that she purchased retained her original tax cost of $18,000 (less depreciation) ; the portion she inherited upon her husband's death was subsequently valued at $30,000 (half of the $60,000 market value at the time he died).

Child-care deduction
This tax break could mean much to a widow who has young children and must work. If she has an adjusted gross income of $35,000 a year or less, she can deduct up to $400 a month for the cost of paying for a babysitter while she goes to work. (This is true for any household—not just a widow's.) That could mean a $4,800 deduction for the year, provided she has paid out in wages the maximum expenditures allowed each month. If the household income is more than $35,000, for every $1 above that amount the deduction is reduced by 50 cents. Thus, at $44,600 eligibility ceases.

The rules are that the dependents must be members of the household and less than fifteen years old or dependent adults who are incapable of caring for themselves. Expenses must be incurred strictly to allow your widow (or wife) to work. She cannot count volunteer work or shopping or entertainment trips. The sitter, maid, mother's helper, or whoever it is, must come to your house unless expenses are for items such as child day-care center costs. A close relative such as a mother-in-law does not qualify. You are allowed to deduct the costs of a person who does your laundry, cleans, cooks, or takes care of other household duties as well as looks after the dependent. "Luxury" wages, such as for a gardener or a chauffeur, do not qualify.

The only time you can deduct for child-care expenses incurred outside the home is if your under-fifteen child is in a day-care center, private nursery school, kindergarten, camp, or after-school play group; or to a baby-sitter in another house.

The maximum you can claim in any month is $400 for care in the home if you have one child, or $200 for care outside. With two children, the maximum outside is $300. For three or more children, you can take off $400 whether the care is in your home or elsewhere. The limit is also $400 for in-the-home expenses when the dependent is an incapacitated adult; and the deduction for him will be reduced if he receives income, even nontaxable income or disability payments.

It is possible to split or combine deductions. Say your widow pays for a maid to come to the house and she also leaves your small children at a child-care center while she works. She could take off $200 for the maid and $200 for the child-care center. Or it might be $200 for the maid, $100 for the child-care center, and $100 a month for a nurse for an incapacitated dependent adult.

There is no way to create a monthly average for this deduction. Even though your widow's child-care expenses were $500 for, say, August and $300 for September, she could take only $400 for August and $300 for September. She cannot average them together to deduct $400 for each month. Also, she is eligible to take deductions only when she is working "substantially full time," which means three-quarters or more of a normal work period. If she does not work full time during some months, she cannot take the deduction during those months.

If your children work

Be sure your wife realizes that, with your steady income gone, it may be necessary for your youngsters to help out with the family finances and college expenses. The tax laws are set up so that anyone can make up to $2,050 in a year without paying tax (the low-income allowance, plus his exemption). He can only use the low-income allowance to offset earned income, however. Any unearned income of a minor from securities or the like is taxable to the extent it exceeds $750.

Even above $2,050, your child's tax probably will be minimal since he is likely to be in a low bracket. What's more, your widow can take him as an exemption on her return even if he has already taken himself on his return—provided she has paid over half his support and, if he is over nineteen, he has been a full-time student for at least five months during the year.

What if your youngster earns quite a bit? Your widow should look over the tax picture toward the end of the year to see if she meets the "over half his support" test. ("Support" generally means food, shelter figured at fair rent value, clothing, transportation, education, medical, recreational, and similar expenses.) When the goal is a bit in doubt, she may want to donate a few extra dollars to his support before the year ends, or have him put some earnings into a savings account rather than spend it on his own support.

Your widow could be entitled to the same deductions as any home-businessman. Suppose she makes and sells clothes, or writes magazine articles for a living. She uses one room of the house exclusively for sewing or for writing, and in size the room is about one-eighth of the house. Provided she uses that space exclusively for her work, she can figure one-eighth of a number of household expenses, such as mortgage payments, cleaning woman, electricity, insurance, and so forth, and deduct it against the amount she earns through the business. This rule-of-thumb also applies in reaching a business deduction if she rents a room to someone. The deduction should reduce the taxes she would have to pay on her profits, and she may even show a loss during some years. In that case, she may be able to take the loss as a deduction on her personal income tax return.

Working at home

What IRS does or does not allow for home-business deductions can get complicated. The government draws a specific line between hobbies and businesses, for instance, and what you can do in each case is spelled out exactly. Also, a taxpayer may not be able to take the full square-footage percentage when the work area is used for other purposes, too. If your widow faces these decisions, she should check with her tax consultant. (His fees are tax-deductible.)

If your widow goes into business for herself, in her home or elsewhere, she might want to set up a "Keogh plan" to provide income for her retirement years. (You can do this for your own part- or full-

time business, too, and you don't have to be in-
corporated.)

The Keogh plan, named after the author of the
1962 act providing for the program, was designed
to give self-employed persons some of the retirement privileges that corporations give their employees. The plan provides a tax shelter in two
ways. Money you put into your retirement fund up
to the yearly maximum allowed is generally not
taxed as current income; and money the fund earns
is sheltered from taxes as the investment grows.

Under present law, you can put 15 percent of
your self-employment income into the plan each
year, but no more than $7,500. There are a variety
of "funding mediums" under Keogh, including
mutual funds, savings accounts, and self-admin-
istered plans arranged through a trustee. Your
bank or lawyer will have details.

Selling the house   This task a widow often faces alone. She may not
want to keep a large home once you and the children
are no longer there. She also may need the money.

Explain these points to your wife: If she sells
before she reaches age sixty-five she will be taxed
on the capital gains realized on any profit unless she
buys a more expensive house within a year, or
builds one within eighteen months. That seems unlikely for a widow who probably is looking for more
modest surroundings. However, if she waits until
she is sixty-five to sell, she may be able to avoid
taxes on part or all of the gain even if she buys a
smaller home or no home at all. Many factors determine the tax, but the fundamental rule is that when
the sales price, minus certain improvement and
selling expenses, is $20,000 or less, the gain is com-

pletely tax-free. Above $20,000, the gain attributable to the first $20,000 of the sales price still is tax-free.

The same applies for you in your retirement years, of course; widows do not have an exclusive right to this privilege. In either case, to qualify you must have owned the house for at least eight years and used it as your main residence for five years or more within that period. You are allowed the tax-exclusion option only once.

10

How to Defend Your Estate

Most of us are constantly aware of income taxes because deductions are made from our paychecks each week. We are less aware of other federal and state taxes because we are confronted with them less frequently. But these taxes, when they strike, can be very painful, particularly when the head of a family dies.

In that event, federal and state governments, in addition to collecting regular income taxes, seek a slice of the estate that is left behind. States take another slice in the form of inheritance taxes levied against beneficiaries of the estate. In addition, governments impose taxes on gifts made by donors while living and on recipients of these gifts.

This makes it essential for husbands, wives, and

members of their family to secure an understanding of the threat which these special taxes represent to the family estate and to their future welfare. Perhaps the most important and the most dangerous is the so-called estate tax.

Your wife should be advised that estate planning is a team effort, carried out by the husband and wife with the help of an attorney experienced in such matters, a qualified life insurance adviser, and in some cases a certified public accountant. In order for any estate plan to be worthwhile it must be understood by the wife and acceptable to her without regard to the tax consequences. The reason for this is that a plan which reduces taxes but does not serve the needs of a widow cannot possibly be a successful plan.

Team needed for estate planning

Before becoming involved in a detailed discussion of estate taxes, it is essential that several principles be clearly fixed in your wife's mind. First, everyone is entitled to an automatic exemption before being required to file a return. Second, a married person may also take advantage of a "marital deduction" and leave an estate of $120,000 not subject to estate tax. While this amount may seem large, in an inflationary period many estates do reach this value.

An estate tax return is required to be filed nine months after the death of an individual whose gross estate is $60,000 or more. The federal tax laws are not concerned with whose names may appear on the title or deed to property, nor the fact that property may be owned jointly with an automatic right of survivorship. If you actually owned the property at the time of your death, it would be

includable in your estate without regard to how the
property is titled. Therefore, you should explain to
your wife that even though your house is owned
jointly, the total value of the house must be included in your gross estate unless she can show that
she has contributed some of her earnings or some
independent wealth or inheritance towards the purchase of your home. This same principle applies to
stocks, bonds, business interests, and any other
asset.

For this reason you and your wife should maintain and preserve a record of what she has contributed to jointly owned property and be in a position
to prove her sources.

**How
records
save
taxes**
The value of records in achieving tax savings can
be seen in this true case history, related by a certified public accountant of Washington, D.C. A husband died, leaving about half a million dollars worth
of stock in a large local corporation and a home
worth about $120,000. It appeared that a substan-
tial tax would be due since the initial presumption
of the Internal Revenue Service is that property in
a husband's name is to be included in his estate and
that the widow, though listed as a joint owner,
must prove that she had contributed to the property before a portion can be excluded. In this particular situation, it was possible to trace the ownership of the corporate stock back to the father of
the widow, who subsequently added her husband's
name to the certificates without formally making
a gift of them to him. Thus, that very large asset
was excluded from the husband's estate and not
subject to tax, even though a full disclosure of the
fact had to be made in the return.

Another important fact came to light when the widow was able to show the entire history of her house. At the time of her marriage, the widow had been working and had accumulated $4,000. This money, in a savings account, was later used as a down payment on a small house in 1926. In the middle thirties, they sold it at a profit and purchased their present house, using the proceeds of the first house as a down payment. Even though the husband had been principal breadwinner of the family and had paid the mortgage payments out of his earnings, the fact that the wife provided the initial funds was sufficient to show that a part of the residence was properly excludable from the husband's gross estate. Fortunately for her, the widow was able to produce the actual bank book, the settlement sheet for the purchase of the first house on which the deposit at the closing exactly matched the withdrawal from the savings account on the same day, as well as the settlement sheet on the sale of the first house and purchase of their final home, showing the transfer of equity from one to the other. This was a case where the records were worth their weight in gold.

You and your wife should understand that certain property, such as real estate, may pass directly to a joint owner under "operation of law," and most states provide that inherited real estate passes directly to the heirs upon a death without having to go through the hands of an executor or administrator. These assets nevertheless become a part of the taxable gross estate.

Certain other assets, such as life insurance, may pass directly to a beneficiary, but they nevertheless may be subject to estate tax. Thus, you might explain to your wife that, unless you transfer ownership of your policies to her, your estate may be taxable on the proceeds of your life insurance. It is also important to explain that it is generally advisable to transfer all "incidents of ownership" and premium payments to her so as to be able to exclude the insurance benefits from your estate.

As we have seen from the foregoing examples, estate taxes and consequently planning to reduce them can be complex. The more a widow knows, the better equipped she is to face the burdens of the administration of an estate and reduce the tax bite. Here is another actual case history which illustrates the advantage that a knowledgeable widow has over one who has no understanding of her late husband's business affairs.

Tom and Ruby Campbell had been married for thirty years. Soon after their marriage, Tom purchased a small printing company which he developed into an enterprise worth about $200,000. Their son liked the family business and became active in it. After a number of years, Tom decided to give his son a substantial interest in the business, and he consulted an attorney. All of the legal requirements were met, including the filing of a gift tax return for the interest in the business given to the son. Since the value was slightly under $60,000 and since Ruby joined in giving the gift, no tax was due on that return.

Within two years disaster struck. Tom became a victim of cancer and died just about two years after having given his son the $60,000 gift. When Ruby was working with the attorneys and accountants for the estate, they explained to her that, since the gift of the stock had been given to the son within three years of his father's death, the Internal Revenue Service would undoubtedly take the position that it was a gift given in "contemplation of death" and, even though it was a valid gift and not subject to probate proceedings, was nevertheless taxable. The advisers estimated that the tax on this single additional item to be included in the estate would be about $15,000.

Ruby found this hard to accept and developed new information. First, the purpose of the gift was to create an incentive for their son and to provide the security that the son desired and was entitled to have. One month after the father gave the son the gift, the father dropped an inexpensive group life insurance plan offered by his trade association for all employees of his company. His only cost was his personal premium of $5.10 per month for $10,000 worth of life insurance. Two months after the date of the gift, a friend in the insurance business approached the father and convinced him to apply for a large life insurance policy. The father passed the physical and the policy was issued, but he rejected it because he "couldn't see spending $1,100 a year for $50,000 worth of life insurance." Finally, the physician's records clearly indicated that the father had had his annual physical one month before the gift to his son and had passed with "flying colors." In this case, the widow's knowledge and ability to prove these facts not only convinced her lawyers and accountants that the gift to their son was not in "contemplation of death," but enabled them to prove it to the government for a net savings of $15,000.

We have seen in the above examples some of the complexities where assets in the husband's name weren't taxed to him, where assets not in the hus-

Widow must know what to tell

band's name could have been taxed to him, and where assets passing directly to the heirs were includable in the taxable estate. In every case, a knowledge of what to tell the professional representatives was important to the widow in order to leave the most dollars after taxes.

Marital deduction   The federal tax laws include a provision known as the "marital deduction," which allows a widow to inherit *tax-free* half of her husband's adjusted gross estate. Such a deduction can take a great deal of the sting out of estate taxes, especially when it is combined with an automatic $60,000 deduction.

There is no question that the marital deduction is easily the most valuable tool available for reducing estate taxes. Prior to 1948, this particular deduction was available only in states having community property laws. In those states, each spouse is considered to own half of all property earned and accumulated during their marriage, and thus only half is subject to tax at the time of the husband's death. The marital deduction was enacted by Congress to equalize this tax situation for citizens of all states.

The rule is that if at least half of an estate is left to a widow only one-half of the total estate is subject to estate tax. In order to qualify for the marital deduction, the amount must be left for the widow in a way which permits her to determine how her share of the estate will be disposed of at her death. Let's look at some examples of the value of the marital deduction.

Albert Wilson died leaving an estate of $500,000. After deducting the specific exemption of $60,000, there was a taxable estate of $440,000. If he left all his property directly to his children rather than to his wife, there would be no marital deduction and the federal and state estate taxes would total about $126,000.

But, if he left his entire estate to his wife, one-half of the estate, or $250,000, would qualify for the marital deduction, so the estate taxes would be only about $47,000, some $79,000 less. However, this would cause another problem: What is the ulti-mate tax on the widow's estate if she survives him for a number of years and is able to keep the entire estate intact by living on the income from the es-tate? If she does not remarry, at the time of her death her estate will be subject to taxes of $110,000, which, when added to the $47,000 her husband paid, increases the total death taxes to $157,000. This is $31,000 greater than the tax would have been if her husband had not provided for the use of the marital deduction in his will. There is a solution through the use of one of several techniques whereby the husband leaves his wife only one-half of his estate and his children or others inherit the other half.

Most husbands take the position that they want to leave their widows as much as possible without regard to the tax savings involved, and this can also be accomplished with good planning. If you leave your widow one-half of your estate outright, it is eligible for the marital deduction. You could even leave it to her in trust, provided the trust on her half of the property gives her the right to invade the principal, to dispose of it in any way that she chooses, and to have the income for life. Of course, this means that eventually it will be taxed in her estate but, since it was not taxed in your estate, this is the best of all possible arrangements.

But what about the second half of the estate

which is not being left outright to the widow? If
the husband chooses to leave this money in trust
for his widow, giving her all of the income during
her lifetime and such principal as trustees may
deem necessary for her support, the second half of
the estate will not be taxable at the time the widow
dies but she will have had the right to the income
until her death.

In the above example, if Albert Wilson left his
wife only half of the estate, and the balance for her
benefit in trust, going to her children after her
death, the tax at the time of the husband's death
would be only $47,000. Assuming that the widow
died ten years later without remarrying, and assuming that she had kept the $250,000 she received
from her husband's estate intact by living only on
the income, it would pass to her children with the
payment of another $47,000 in taxes. Thus, the
combined tax would be $94,000, some $63,000 less
than would be paid had the widow received the entire taxable estate, lived on the income, and passed
it along to her children. This is an illustration of
effective estate planning that must be done *before*
the husband dies.

Sometimes it happens that wives resent being
left only half of a husband's estate, not realizing
the tremendous impact this type of planning could
have on the ultimate tax paid after both have died.
If the wife knows that she will have the income
from the entire estate and the right to invade principal whenever necessary, she will usually accept
this arrangement and be happy to pass along the
very substantial savings as a bonus to her children.

In thinking about the marital deduction, keep in
mind that any property includable in your estate
which goes to your wife is part of the marital de-

duction. This means that life insurance proceeds, a home jointly owned which she takes by right of survivorship, and jointly owned bank accounts qualify as assets under the marital deduction. But also remember, if you and your wife own everything jointly, it is like leaving your entire estate to her and can therefore be subject to a double tax. This is the big problem with jointly held property; all of it will be included in her estate, which will incur a substantial tax cost.

Make sure a "common disaster" clause is included in your will to cover the problem that arises when a married couple is in a fatal accident together and it is difficult to determine who died first. In such cases, the law presumes the husband survived the wife, and no marital deduction is allowed since, so the law reasons, he died as a widower. The common disaster clause avoids this problem by declaring that in such a circumstance the husband will be presumed to have died first. Thus, the wife will inherit the husband's property in the eyes of the law, and the estate will benefit from the marital deduction. *Her* estate will not, of course, but the savings in taxes can amount to thousands of dollars.

"Common disaster" provision

There is a special relief provision of the law which provides some benefit when assets are inherited by an individual after the payment of taxes and the inheritor subsequently dies. Assets which have previously been taxed in an estate are eligible for a special credit. The credit is determined on the length of time since the previous death and is reduced from 80 percent in the first year to 20 percent in the tenth year.

Because of the inflationary times in which we

live, it is important that a review of your estate
plan be made at least every three years. Not only
should you give consideration to changes in your
family such as the number of children, their ages
and education, but the changes in valuation of your
property. It is not uncommon that a house bought
ten years ago for $25,000 is worth $60,000 today.
Some investment property purchased a few years
ago for a very small sum could be worth many times
the original cost. Remember, it is the fair market
value at the date of death that is the value upon
which the estate tax is usually based. (However, to
protect against market value fluctuations and other
factors, there is a special alternative valuation date
of six months after the date of death which might
be useful in some cases.)

There are some other estate planning techniques
which might apply to you and which you might
wish to discuss with your wife. For instance, if you
have a sizable estate and want to increase the size
of your marital deduction to give you greater flexibility in the amount you leave your widow and your
overall estate planning, you could purchase a large
life insurance policy payable to your estate, and
then provide a bequest in your will to your favorite
charity for the amount of the proceeds of the life
insurance. In this way you would increase your
gross estate by the amount of the insurance, but
not your taxable estate since the bequest to the
charity would bring it down to where it would have
been otherwise. However, since the gross estate
would be increased, you could increase the amount
you leave your widow under the marital deduction
provisions which escape taxes entirely.

It sometimes happens that individuals who have
large investments in assets that are not readily sal-

able are unable to pay estate taxes when they become due. For instance, someone who owns a large
percentage of the stock in a closely held company of
substantial value could find it difficult to provide
enough liquidity in his estate to meet immediate
needs and to pay taxes. Recognizing this, Congress
has provided two important special payment provisions in the estate tax law which might be an important part of your planning. One provision allows
a ten-year payoff on the installment method with
four percent interest for that part of estate taxes
attributable to the ownership of a large percentage
of a family business which is a substantial portion
of your estate. Another provision permits an estate
to request a period of up to three years for defer-
ring tax payment because of the inability to dispose
of assets without sacrificing them due to temporary
market conditions. To qualify for *either* provision,
the application for relief must be made at the time
of filing tax returns for the estate.

In addition to the federal tax, most states assess **Inheritance**
taxes upon those who inherit wealth. Federal laws **taxes**
provide a credit against the estate tax for the
amount of inheritance taxes paid. Although sometimes the inheritance tax is less or greater than the
allowance, in most cases the effective inheritance
tax is the amount allowed as a credit on the federal
return and thus there is no additional cost incurred
by the inheritance tax.

Next to the judicious use of the marital deduc- **Giving**
tion, the best estate planning technique involves **while**
the giving of gifts. For estate tax planning pur- **living**

How to Compute Gross Estate Tax

Taxable estate equal to or more than—	Taxable estate less than—	Tax on amount in column (1)	Rate of tax on excess over amount in column (1)
(1)	**(2)**	**(3)**	**(4)**
			Percent
0	$5,000	0	3
$5,000	10,000	$150	7
10,000	20,000	500	11
20,000	30,000	1,600	14
30,000	40,000	3,000	18
40,000	50,000	4,800	22
50,000	60,000	7,000	25
60,000	100,000	9,500	28
100,000	250,000	20,700	30
250,000	500,000	65,700	32
500,000	750,000	145,700	35
750,000	1,000,000	233,200	37
1,000,000	1,250,000	325,700	39
1,250,000	1,500,000	423,200	42
1,500,000	2,000,000	528,200	45
2,000,000	2,500,000	753,200	49
2,500,000	3,000,000	998,200	53
3,000,000	3,500,000	1,263,200	56
3,500,000	4,000,000	1,543,200	59
4,000,000	5,000,000	1,838,200	63
5,000,000	6,000,000	2,468,200	67
6,000,000	7,000,000	3,138,200	70
7,000,000	8,000,000	3,838,200	73
8,000,000	10,000,000	4,568,200	76
10,000,000	. . . .	6,088,200	77

Source: Internal Revenue Service

How to Compute Federal Gift Tax

Amount of taxable gifts equal to or more than— (A)	Amount of taxable gifts less than— (B)	Tax on amount in column (A) (C)	Rate of tax on access over amount in column (A) (D)
			Percent
0	$5,000	0	2¼
5,000	10,000	$112.50	5¼
10,000	20,000	375.00	8¼
20,000	30,000	1,200.00	10½
30,000	40,000	2,250.00	13½
40,000	50,000	3,600.00	16½
50,000	60,000	5,250.00	18¾
60,000	100,000	7,125.00	21
100,000	250,000	15,525.00	22½
250,000	500,000	49,275.00	24
500,000	750,000	109,275.00	26¼
750,000	1,000,000	174,900.00	27¾
1,000,000	1,250,000	244,275.00	29¼
1,250,000	1,500,000	317,400.00	31½
1,500,000	2,000,000	396,150.00	33¾
2,000,000	2,500,000	564,900.00	36¾
2,500,000	3,000,000	748,650.00	39¾
3,000,000	3,500,000	947,400.00	42
3,500,000	4,000,000	1,157,400.00	44¼
4,000,000	5,000,000	1,378,650.00	47¼
5,000,000	6,000,000	1,851,150.00	50¼
6,000,000	7,000,000	2,353,650.00	52½
7,000,000	8,000,000	2,878,650.00	54¾
8,000,000	10,000,000	3,426,150.00	57
10,000,000	. . . .	4,566,150.00	57¾

Source: Internal Revenue Service

poses, the giving of a gift that will remove an asset from your estate means relinquishing all current and future interest in the property. If you give a gift without strings attached more than three years before you die, the property will not be included in your estate. While there is a tax that the gift-giver must pay, the gift tax is lower than the estate tax.

A separate set of exemptions applies to the gift tax. The law permits you to give an annual gift of up to $3,000 to each of as many persons as you wish without paying gift tax. This giving does not affect your current income tax but it can substantially reduce future estate taxes. In addition to these annual allowances, you have a lifetime allowance of $30,000 for giving tax-free gifts. Of even greater significance is the fact that a wife can join with her husband in making a gift, thereby increasing the annual exemptions to $6,000 for each individual to whom you wish to give a gift, and raising the lifetime allowance to $60,000.

After these allowances have been used, each time taxable gifts are given the tax is computed on the accumulated value of the taxable gifts that have been given in your lifetime. Since the gift tax, like estate and income taxes, increases as the taxable amount increases, this "accumulation factor" means that the greater the taxable giving the greater the tax. Several years ago Congress changed the gift tax laws to require the filing of gift tax returns on a quarterly rather than an annual basis. The avowed reason for doing so was to expedite the collection of tax revenues. This may give you some idea of the popularity of the giving of gifts, even taxable gifts, as part of estate planning.

Gift taxes are approximately only three-quarters of the amount of the federal estate tax on the same property. This savings, in addition to the annual and lifetime gift tax exclusions, is illustrated in the following example.

Bill and Peggy Evans are married and have two children. They have accumulated an estate valued at $300,000, all includable in Bill's estate tax return. His will provides that at his death his estate will be divided so that one-half goes to his wife and one-quarter to each child. At Bill's death, the total estate tax will be $17,900.

Change the facts so that Bill gives half of his estate away in one year—one-fourth to his wife and one-eighth to each child. At his death he leaves the remainder to his family in the same proportions. The estate tax incurred at his death would be $880 after having paid a gift tax of $3,094, for a total of $3,974. This is a savings of $13,926!

Now let's again change the facts and have Bill give a large part of his estate away. In one year he makes gifts of $66,000 to his wife and $6,000 to his two children. In each of the next six years, he gives $6,000 to his wife and children. At death, he leaves half of the remaining estate to his wife and half to his children. The result is that at his death he will have paid neither estate nor gift taxes!

Of course, this illustration is based on the presumption that the gifts were not classed as gifts "in contemplation of death" and thus includable in his estate, and on the assumption that Bill was willing to give away almost all of his assets.

If a husband initiates a gift program, files gift tax returns, and pays the tax in the three-year period before his death, and the Internal Revenue Service takes the position that the gifts were in contemplation of death and thus includable in his estate tax return, nothing is lost. The estate is then entitled to a full credit for the gift taxes paid for assets which are subsequently included in the donor's estate tax return.

You should not enter into the giving of substantial gifts without an evaluation of the entire program with your professional advisers. It is important that certain prescribed methods of gift-giving be followed and that a careful evaluation be made of your assets to ensure that you and your family are protected against potential misfortune and not exposed to possible poverty because of your desire to avoid estate taxes.

Another tax-saving possibility   Sometimes an individual is unwilling or unable to make taxable gifts to reduce his estate. This could be due to the fact that a gift given by someone who is elderly or in poor health would very likely come under the "contemplation of death" rules, or it may be because a person feels he needs the income. In cases of this sort there is a worthwhile method of reducing estate taxes through the purchase of certain types of U.S. government bonds which are sold at a discount but which can be used at their full face value to pay estate taxes. They can usually be purchased through a bank or stockbroker.

These so-called "flower bonds" usually bear interest at a low rate, and some of them are not due for another twenty or thirty years. These two factors cause the bonds to be sold at substantially less than their full face value. For instance, some bonds paying 3½ percent interest, due in 1988, are selling today at about 75 percent of their full face value. Even though the bond bears a stated interest rate of only $3\frac{1}{2}$ percent, remember that you are paying only 75 percent of the full face price, thus increasing your yield to about 5 percent. The following true story may be an example of "late stage" planning, but certainly illustrates a point.

Late one Friday night a certified public accountant received a phone call from a client. It seems that the client's mother-in-law, an elderly woman, had become seriously ill and was rushed to the hospital. She was not expected to live much longer. The mother-in-law and her daughters had about $300,-000 in joint savings accounts, all of which would be subject to estate tax in the mother's hands. The purpose of the phone call was to find out from the accountant what, if anything, could be done to reduce estate taxes. The accountant explained that removing the money from the savings accounts at that late date would certainly not exclude the amount from the woman's estate. Then he told his client about "flower bonds." The mother-in-law was still alive on Monday morning when her daughters bought her $65,000 worth of "flowers" for $48,750. The mother lived about two more weeks and the $65,000 worth of bonds were almost exactly enough to pay off the federal estate tax in full, a savings of $16,250.

In order to qualify for this special provision, the bonds must be of a certain issue qualifying for this purpose and they must have been owned by the deceased during his lifetime (or in a trust includable in his estate).

There is one more gift tax technique which is worth your consideration. It has previously been mentioned that in cases where the husband is the principal earner but has placed their house in his wife's name, the residence will nevertheless be included in the husband's estate. You could take advantage of a special provision of the Internal Revenue Code which permits a husband to consider the inclusion of his wife as a joint owner of their residence as a taxable gift even though usually no tax will result. If this is done, half of the increase in the value of the house will be excluded from the husband's estate, which can be of significant estate tax savings in these days of rapid inflation.

No discussion about gift taxes would be complete without a warning of the problem that could arise from placing bank accounts and securities in joint names. The mere placing of your wife's name on a joint bank account is not in and of itself a gift. The same is true when you take your income and purchase securities jointly. The only time it becomes a taxable gift is when your wife exercises her rights with regard to that joint account, such as taking the money and converting it to her own use. This is illustrated in the following example.

Harry Gordon saves $10,000 of his salary and puts it in a savings account. As a matter of convenience, he adds his wife's name as a joint owner of the account. There is no tax implication in this act. However, his wife, Beverly, subsequently withdraws $9,000 and purchases securities in *her* name. This act creates a taxable gift and initiates the need for the filing of a gift tax return.

Property in trust   During the past decade, many persons have become interested in the technique of using trusts. Property placed in trust could bypass estate probate proceedings which *may* exclude it from your taxable estate. Another common type of trust could exclude the income from the property in the trust

from your personal income tax return. Your wife
should understand what a trust is if you plan to
use one.

A trust can most simply be described as an arrangement whereby legal title is transferred to
another person or to a trust company, with instructions for the trustee to hold, invest, and administer
the property for the benefit of the persons designated in the trust agreement. The person who creates the trust agreement is known as the creator,
settlor, grantor, or donor; the holder of the legal
title who is instructed to act under the terms of the
trust agreement is called the trustee; the person
who receives the benefits from the trust is called
the beneficiary; and the individual or institution to
whom the balance of the trust is distributed at the
end of the trust period is called the remainder man.

A living trust can be used by an individual who
wishes to divest himself of certain income but does
not wish to give up the asset which creates the income for life. This is sometimes called a Clifford
trust and is illustrated by the following example.

Living trusts

Ken Martin is married with two children. He is
in the 50 percent tax bracket and owns a piece of
property which gives him about $3,000 a year tax-
able income. He has only $1,500 of this income left
after paying taxes. He creates a Clifford-type trust
for the benefit of his two children with instructions
that the income be paid to them for the next eleven
years. This will help pay for their education and
assist them during their early years after college.
The trustees are instructed to make annual distri-
butions of income to the children. The tax conse-
quence is that for eleven years the income from that

property will be distributed to his children and be taxed at their very low rate. At the ehd of the eleven-year period, the property will revert to Ken Martin, who may need that income in his retirement or for his widow.

There are many other examples of living trusts that can be established to serve the purpose of having an independent party, the trustee, carry out your instructions during and after your lifetime, with various effects. For instance, Charles Brady is rather well fixed. His will leaves more than adequate assets to provide income for his wife after his death. He is interested in reducing his taxes and diverting some income to his daughter, Mary. He creates a $50,000 trust, using his lawyer as trustee, with the understanding that his daughter is to receive the income from the trust until her thirty-first birthday, after which the entire sum is to be distributed to her without restrictions. Since he has given up all rights and interest in the money, it would be excludable from his estate unless he dies within three years of creating the trust, in which case the "contemplation of death" question could be raised by the government. However, since he has made an absolute gift to his daughter, a gift tax would be due at the time the money is put into the trust.

Swindlers prey on widows   You could provide for a trust in your will with your wife as beneficiary. Even though she may have a right to ultimately dispose of the funds in the trust in her own will, there is some measure of protection for her since it is unlikely that a trustee would give her a large sum of money from the principal unless there is an absolutely justifiable reason.

Unfortunately, many widows are not able to protect themselves from unscrupulous individuals who attempt to fleece them of their nest eggs by a number of methods. In other instances the widow loses her nest egg when she and the person to whom she gives money are acting with the best of intentions. For example, three years after the death of her husband, who left her his entire estate outright in her own name, a widow became friendly with a man and contemplated remarriage. Her prospective husband was a decent individual, honest and kind. Unfortunately, however, he was the owner of a small business which was in financial trouble.

Shortly before their marriage, the widow questioned her fiancé about his obvious anxiety. He admitted that he needed $20,000 to save his business. The widow tried to help him and invested more and more in the business, which nevertheless failed. She ultimately lost all the financial security her first husband had left her. Had her husband left this money to her in trust, the trustees certainly would not have permitted this type of transaction and could have preserved her inheritance for her. What may have been equally important to her, she would not have been the person to deny her prospective husband the loan; it would have been the trustees, such as a bank or a law firm, who would have weighed it on a cold businesslike basis.

Then there was the case of a widow who acted to protect herself after her late husband had failed to do so. She received several hundred thousand dollars as the beneficiary of her husband's estate. Lacking any business experience or knowledge, she could easily have been the target for a swindler or for someone whom she would have found it hard to refuse a loan, such as a prospective husband.

Her attorney suggested that she place all her money in trust at a bank with instructions for them to pay out a certain amount to her every year with the balance, if any, going to her designated heirs after her death. She could retain the right to redistribute amongst the heirs or could forego the right to make changes, although some small gift tax problems would arise in the latter arrangement.

It was a wise widow who accepted this recommendation from her lawyer and placed the property in trust. She could arrange to have either a specific amount paid out each year or have the amount designated in accordance with the cost of living and provide that the trustees could pay a greater amount from the principal in the event of an emergency or medical needs.

Consider trusts carefully
Never attempt to establish a trust without competent professional legal advice. Careful consideration should be given to the selection of a trustee. Obviously, the trustee should not be one who has an interest, either current or future, in the property. You should also beware of tying up property so tightly that you cannot have the use of the money in case of need.

The term of a trust is usually limited to the lifetime of one person, plus twenty-one years. After the maximum period expires, the trust is terminated and the property is distributed in accordance with the terms of the trust.

Be sure there is an understanding with the trustees about fees. Commercial trustees' fees can vary and should be agreed upon in advance. An individual's fee for acting as trustee is a matter of agreement between the parties, and the trustee is always entitled to be reimbursed for costs, such as legal fees and bonds.

Income earned by your estate after your death or by a trust created during your lifetime or under the terms of your will must be accounted for in tax returns and in some cases taxes must be paid on it. An estate is entitled to a $600 exemption and a trust to a $100 exemption. The net income after deductions is subject to tax at the same tax rate that applies to unmarried individuals. If the income from the estate or trust is distributed to a beneficiary, the individual who received the money is taxed and not the estate or trust. If items that are taxed in a special manner, such as capital gains, are earned by an estate or trust and distributed to a beneficiary, the same advantageous form of taxing is passed along to the individual.

Income tax on estates and trusts

11

Your Most Important Papers

Even though you have spent much time going over your financial affairs with your wife, you should prepare a summary to be read at the time of your death. This is what lawyers call "a last letter of instructions." It is not a legally binding document, as your will is meant to be, but the letter will be of great help to your widow at a time when she will need all the help she can get.

For one thing, such a letter gives you a chance to communicate with her in an informal, loving way— person-to-person, in the language of a letter. For another, you will be providing her with an easy-to-follow list to use and share with others who will be trying to help.

Make sure there is a copy of your letter in a place

where your widow or executor can get it quickly. If
you would prefer to have it remain sealed until your
death, leave it with your lawyer, and let your wife
know it is there. Or keep it in a home strong box,
marked "Letter of last instructions of John R. Doe,
to his wife Mary. Not to be opened until the death
of John R. Doe." Don't keep the only copy of the letter in your safe deposit box, even if you co-own it
with your wife; you will want her to have immediate access to the letter, and the box may be sealed
by the state for a few days.

Here are some suggestions about what information to include in your letter of last instructions.

Important points to include

Location of your will. Where can every copy be
found? Where is the signed original? What are the
names and addresses of all executors, trustees,
lawyers, or guardians involved? Are there any pe-
culiar provisions in your will that you would like to
explain in simple language here?

The experts in your life. Although you should
have seen to it that your wife has become ac-
quainted with those people most directly involved
in your personal business affairs, it will be helpful
to provide a list of their names and addresses. Include your lawyer, stockbroker, banker, business
associates, accountant, real estate broker, and anyone else of that nature.

Your safe deposit box. Where is it located? Who
is authorized by the bank to open it? What are its
contents? Where is the key?

Your essential personal papers. Where are your
marriage and birth certificates? Copies of adoption
proceedings for any adopted children? Military
service papers? Evidence of divorce or separation?

Citizenship papers? Social Security card? Auto registration?

All people who should be notified. In addition to the experts mentioned earlier, what are the names, addresses, and phone numbers of your parents, as well as other relatives or friends you would want to be notified? Also put down the pertinent information about your present employer and close associates at work.

Burial instructions. Where is the family burial plot? The deed? What sort of funeral arrangements do you want? (Again, this is an uncomfortable subject to discuss with your wife, but it is essential for her to understand your wishes. This letter will help with the details.)

Also provide insurance information

Life insurance policies. How much? What companies? Who are the beneficiaries? Names of your agents? Where are the policies kept? Where are your premium receipts and dividend statements? Any loans against your policies? Any annuity contracts? If so, where are they? What about company group insurance? Are there special provisions if death occurs while you are traveling on business (many company plans pay double)? Do you own a policy on anyone else's life? A key point: what should your beneficiaries do with the insurance checks?

Medical or disability insurance. What and where are these policies? (There may be provisions to cover final illness bills that otherwise would be charged to the estate.) If they cover other family members, how will this coverage be affected?

All your cash accounts. That means numbers and locations of checking as well as savings—jointly or personally held, and the savings accounts pass-books. Any certificates of deposit? Cash in your safe deposit box or business safe? Most important: where can your wife or executor get ready cash for immediate expenses?

Past employment records, current affiliations. You should give places, names of employers, and dates of all employment. What employee-benefit programs have you belonged to? That includes group insurance plans, retirement funds, profit-sharing plans. What about unions or fraternal organizations (there may be death benefits or bur-ial expenses)? Do you have proof of membership in these?

Your military service. Proof of service and/or discharge can be essential. Where are the appropri-ate papers? The Veterans Administration pays some burial fees. And if you were disabled during service, there could be special benefits—educa-tional, among others—for your family.

Tax returns. You should have them—federal, state, and local—for the past six years. Also, where are canceled checks showing payment of taxes? Other supporting documents? Copies of any gift tax returns that have been filed?

Securities. A detailed list is important for all stocks and bonds you own, with titles, certificate numbers, quantities, and the name in which each certificate is registered. Where do you keep them? When did you buy them? For how much? Who is your stockbroker? Have you ever pledged stock as security for a loan? Distinguish stocks bought by you from stocks bought by your wife. The same goes for securities bought for your youngsters and registered in their names. How about U.S. savings bonds? Who are the beneficiaries?

Real estate. Whatever the property—your home, a second home, rental property, undeveloped land— where is it located, what is it like, what is its approximate value, where is the deed? Is there a mortgage? What bank holds it? Where are the papers and what are the monthly payments? Do you have decreasing term life insurance to cover your mortgage (so that the debt would be wiped out upon your death)? Where are other papers: title abstracts, insurance policies (title and homeowner's), surveys, real estate tax receipts, leases, building cost figures, etc.? Who are your real estate and insurance brokers?

Debts owed and owing. Do you have any personal debts outstanding? With whom? Are there regular payments? How about a lump-sum repayment arrangement upon a certain date? Who owes you money? Are there any debts you want to forgive upon your death? (If these are sizable, check with your lawyer about the tax implications.)

Your personal property. Where are the title and registration of your car, and how should transfer of ownership be handled (if not jointly owned)? For specific valuables, such as electronic equipment or jewelry, give details of insurance coverage. Who is the broker? What property is jointly owned?

Trust funds. Are any in effect now? Have you arranged for any in your will? Outline all the provisions and your reasons for setting up the trusts. Who are the trustees? Lawyer? Are you a beneficiary of any trusts yourself? Are there trusts other people have set up under which your family members are beneficiaries?

Charge cards and charge accounts. List all charge cards you own, with numbers and addresses of the companies. That includes bank cards, oil cards, and travel and entertainment cards. Give the same information for any charge accounts you have, whether at stores, clubs, or restaurants.

The location of the papers mentioned above and information about the key people in your business and personal life are essential facts to have on hand at all times. The checklist in Appendix IV may be useful for organizing the material to be included with your letter of last instructions, with copies for your home files and your safe deposit box.

As a general rule, keep irreplaceable documents and records in a safe deposit box. That includes securities, deeds and titles to property, loan notes (for money owed to you), identification papers, and so forth. The exception, as noted before, is the signed copy of your will. This should be kept with your lawyer or in some other secure place, for ready access.

In your home files—preferably a fireproof strong box or filing cabinet—keep complete records of what is in your safe deposit box, a list of credit card numbers, insurance records, and so forth. It is possible to keep actual insurance policies there, too, although many people prefer to keep the originals in their safe deposit boxes. Just be sure you have a working record of all such documents on hand for reference and ready action.

Set up a system for records

One final suggestion: if you haven't already set up your papers and records according to some system like the one suggested in this chapter, get to it right away. Be sure to involve your wife fully in the project. It is an excellent way to familiarize her with your overall finances, as well as with the requirements of record-keeping for sound money

management. If you already have such a system, review it with her. And keep yourself open to suggested changes. A system, after all, isn't a system
unless more than one person can relate to it with
thorough understanding and facility. You both
have to comprehend—and agree to—the methods.

12

When
Death
Strikes

It is not accidental that almost all human societies have a period of mourning.

Your death will generate intense emotions in your wife. She will be abandoned, physically and psychologically. She will be overcome by pain and depression. She will experience tears and numbness and fear. And there will be choked-up anger at the unfairness of the fate that has befallen her.

Your wife will be plunged into a severe identity crisis. True, relatives, friends, business associates, and neighbors can help. Your lawyer, accountant, and many others will provide comfort and advice. But, despite all such empathy and counsel, she will stand alone in a way that she never has as your wife.

**Immediate
tasks
your widow
will face**

At this time, your widow will probably be least capable emotionally of coping with the tasks that face her. Knowing in advance what they will be may help.

1. Your lawyer should be contacted immediately to help handle the many details (financial and otherwise) that must be dealt with. Your will and other important documents must be located and studied, as discussed in the previous chapter.

2. Unless a checking or savings account provides a sufficient amount of ready cash, more money must be found. There are likely to be many demands for cash in the days that follow. Funeral directors are not always willing to wait for payment, for instance. How much cash she will need altogether depends upon a number of factors, such as what kind of funeral, or how elaborate a memorial stone is chosen. Probably at least $2,000 in cash will be required within the first few days.

3. Your clergyman must be contacted and asked to help with arrangements. He also may provide moral support for your wife.

4. Funeral arrangements must be made. Usually this will entail a discussion with a funeral director. Hopefully, you will have left some guidelines in a last letter of instructions, as outlined in the last chapter. Otherwise, your wife must make the decisions—or turn the matter over to someone else. A casket must be chosen. Unless you have decided in advance where you want to be buried, your widow must select a site. The cost may range from very little to several thousand dollars, depending on the locality, the size of the plot, and whether it is a simple piece of land or a vault. The time and place, as well as the character of the ceremony, must be determined.

In some places, the cost of a casket is a gauge in determining the costs of other services. The more expensive the casket, the higher the cost of everything else. Different fabrics, woods, and metals can significantly change the price. (You can get a simple pine box for about $100, although most funeral homes won't make this readily known.) The purchase of an outer receptacle for the coffin also can affect the price tag.

What is true of caskets is also true about markers and other memorials. Too often, a casket and marker are chosen when the widow is filled with pain and grief. As a result, she spends more than she can afford—more than you would ever want her to spend. Other costs that can add up: fees for the minister; masses; music; pallbearers, if friends are not at hand to carry the coffin; limousines; flowers; acknowledgments, which are often printed if the funeral is a large one with many flowers or contributions to favored charities. Although prices vary considerably around the country, this will give you an idea:

The costs can be high

Coffin: Anywhere from less than $200 to more than $8,000. Average cost: about $950.

Services: Flowers, clergyman, honorariums, publication of death notices in local papers, church offerings, clothing for the deceased, transportation, rental of funeral parlor space, certified death transcripts, and so forth. Total cost depends upon the number of services included. A reasonable range would be $250 to $300.

Opening the grave: This is determined by union scale. For planning purposes, an average cost of about $200 seems reasonable.

Cemetery plot: As with all "real estate," location and size are the factors that determine price. Costs vary enormously. An average range: $200 to $500.

Cremation: A coffin often is required for cremation. Even if it is not, you may want one for a viewing. In that case, you might be able to rent one from the funeral director. His services overall can be expected to cost about the same as for a traditional funeral. Probably transportation costs will go up, since a crematorium usually is farther away than a cemetery. Typically, a cremation can cost about $100. There also will be quite a range of prices for the urn.

Transportation of remains: When a body must be taken to another place for burial, a number of additional costs are involved. Included are a shipping case (about $500) and actual transportation charges, which are set by regulatory agencies. If the body is to be shipped by railroad, it is necessary to purchase a coach ticket for the corpse, in addition to paying freight charges. Anyone accompanying the body must buy an extra ticket. If sent by air, the body can be shipped by air freight.

Add it together, and you reach a total of between $500 and $3,000 or more. A median of $1,750 would be reasonable.

5. Your widow will need several copies of a number of different papers. The following should be located rapidly and acted upon immediately:

• *Death certificate.* A widow needs legal proof of her husband's death almost everywhere she turns. She will need a death certificate to establish claims under life insurance policies, veterans' benefits, and Social Security. Usually, the funeral director provides certified copies of the certificate, and your widow simply can request extra copies. Additional certified copies can be ordered for a nominal fee from the office of the registrar of vital statistics for the town or city in which the husband died. Your widow should have a minimum of ten copies.

• *Birth certificate.* This also is needed to substantiate several claims. It is wise to obtain additional copies.

• *Marriage certificate.* Again, several copies will be needed to establish a number of claims. Get one or two with the official seal, and zerox the rest.

• *Your Social Security number and other related information.* Benefits under Social Security do not begin automatically. Delay in making application can cause a loss of some benefits because back payments cannot be made for any period greater than twelve months. Also, there will be up to $255 in death benefits. Your wife could save considerable time by bringing this information to your nearest Social Security office: death certificate; your Social Security number; your employer's name and address and your approximate earnings during the year of your death; W-2 forms for the previous year in which you worked; marriage certificate; her own Social Security number and your children's numbers; proof of her age and the ages of your children who are under twenty-three.

Even if she cannot find every document, your widow should make application immediately. The Social Security office will help her by designating alternate papers she can submit to support her case.

• If you are a veteran, see that your service discharge papers are readily accessible. At the least, your wife should know your service serial number and the branch and dates of your service. Veterans'

Benefits for veterans' widows

benefits available to your wife vary in terms of the extent to which your death resulted from a service-connected cause. If you die from an injury sustained in the service, she is entitled to special benefits. She also gets such benefits if you die on active duty, or within 120 days after discharge from a service-connected cause.

Even if you have been discharged and your death has nothing whatsoever to do with a service-incurred injury, she is entitled to a maximum of $250 for burial expenses. Also, if she wishes, she will be given an American flag with which to drape your coffin. And you can be buried in any national cemetery where there still is room. The exception is the cemetery in Arlington, Virginia; burial there requires meeting specific criteria. This burial benefit includes the grave site and actual interment—that is, opening, closing, and marking of the grave. Even if you are not buried in a national cemetery, a memorial marker or headstone is provided on request from the Department of the Army, no matter what branch of the armed forces you were in. The marker will be shipped to the grave without charge. Your local VA office will tell your widow how to order the marker.

Usually, the funeral director will notify the Veterans Administration when VA insurance is involved. If he does not, your widow should contact the nearest VA center herself, or have your lawyer do it. A local veterans' organization, such as the American Legion, can tell you where to write or call. To make any inquiry about VA insurance, your widow should submit your complete name and your government life insurance policy number.

There are a number of other benefits available to widows of former servicemen. If you have a 100-

percent service-connected disability, your widow
will be entitled to a ten-point preference when she
applies for a Civil Service job—provided she has
not remarried. Similarly, unremarried widows of
men who served in World War II, Korea, or the
post-Korea period, and who died in service or as
a result of a service-connected disability may qualify for GI home loans.

In some cases, your widow and children may be
eligible for financial aid for education under the
War Orphans' and Widows' Educational Assistance Act. For widows, the period of eligibility generally extends for eight years. For children, it usually applies from age eighteen through twenty-five.
Under this act, a widow and each of her children
can receive up to thirty-six months of schooling or
the equivalent if enrolled part time. One excellent
source of information about such educational financing and scholarship possibilities is the annually revised booklet "Need A Lift?" published by
the American Legion. Contact your local branch to
obtain a copy.

**Eligibility
for
education
aid**

6. Your life insurance agent or the company's
home office should be contacted as soon as possible.
Usually, proof of the claim requires only two pieces
of paper: a death certificate or the attending physician's statement; and a statement of claim. The
actual policy is not necessary, since the company's
records will show that the policy exists and what
its status is.

Any claimant also should provide several facts:
policy number and amount; name and address of
the deceased; where and when he last worked;
where and when he was born; date, place, and cause

of death; claimant's full name, address, age, and Social Security number; and possibly a list of other policies.

Whoever makes the claim must show in what capacity he is acting—as beneficiary, executor of your estate, assignee, administrator, or trustee. If you have left the proceeds of a policy to a minor child or to an adult who is incompetent, a guardian must file. When the insurance goes directly to your estate, your administrator or executor is the one to make the claim. In each case, the person must show a certificate of appointment.

Your widow may have the choice of receiving the proceeds in a lump sum or in some other form of payment. Since the time may not be opportune for making up her mind, she might ask to delay this decision a bit. She could ask the company for an amount to cover immediate expenses, then put the rest under an interest option with the understanding that she can withdraw any or all of it later. Thus, the money will begin earning money, and she will be spared making a decision under pressure.

7. Your employer should be notified immediately, so that procedures can begin about any company insurance policies, vested retirement plans, or investment plans. Also, tax and Social Security records must be gathered and copies made. Fraternal and other organizations to which you belong should also be notified; there may be specific benefits available to your widow.

8. As soon as any property held in joint tenancy is cleared to give your widow full title, she should change your fire or other insurance policies immediately to reflect the new ownership situation. As for title to the family car, procedures vary. She should inquire at the local motor vehicle department.

9. Anyone connected with your family's finances should be notified soon. That includes the bank—especially if there are trust arrangements—and your stockbroker. Your widow will have time to sit down with them later, but they should be told of your death immediately. If you live in a state where safe deposit boxes are completely sealed, or bank accounts frozen, your widow should make an immediate request for clearance with the state tax authorities. Usually, the bank cannot process such matters itself; your lawyer should take charge.

In certain areas, some banks provide what is called a "Survivor's Optional Benefits" program to help a widow locate funds and determine certain rights she may not be aware of. For instance, many widows continue to pay installment debts and mortgages, even though there was credit life insurance that would have covered the debts. Such bank services also will provide help in tracking down Social Security and other benefits.

10. As soon as possible, and probably with the help of your lawyer, executor, or other adviser and friend, your wife should gather and list all current bills you owed and amounts of money owed to you. This information will be needed when your estate goes through probate, and in the meantime there may be specific action to take, such as establishing that credit life insurance has met the obligation of certain debts. Your widow should *not* pay off any bills before probate proceedings start, however, with the exception of a few death-related costs.

Clearing probate

Probate is the procedure required by law to see that all your property is protected and distributed properly, and that all your creditors—and the tax men—are paid off appropriately. With small estates, the procedure takes very little time. With larger estates, where taxes will likely be due, it can take quite a bit longer, but rarely more than thirteen months from the date of death.

Here is what your widow will have to do: About a week or ten days following your death, she will go to the probate court with your lawyer. He will know what documents are needed, but certainly they include a copy of the marriage certificate, with information about any previous marriages; the names and addresses of your children; your will, if there is one; and a general picture, to the best of her knowledge, of your total assets.

Then the court will publish in local newspapers a notice that anyone to whom you owe money has three months from the date of the notice to present claims against your estate. These are claims that were incurred before your death, and if your widow is in doubt about any claim, she should refer it to your lawyer. The only other payments that should be made would be for the expenses of your final illness, settling funeral costs, and local taxes; these expenses take precedence over other claims.

Once probate proceedings are begun, your executor will take full charge, and your widow can relax unless she wishes to be actively involved in the proceedings, or she has been named an executor. It is important that you discuss that possibility with your wife at the present time to determine how much she will want to be involved with the actual estate settlement, bearing in mind that she will be very much occupied in pulling her life together and concentrating again on the business of living.

CHAPTER 13

Getting Things Going Again

"It does take time. There was a period there when I thought I'd never become un-numb. But all at once you're ready to start up again, do things, get involved with the kids and see friends. I just couldn't stay dead myself forever."

So a widow in Minneapolis reported her new life to a group of widows, widowers, and divorced parents who met regularly to discuss their problems and plan social activities together. Certainly her experience was typical of many.

How long it takes to get things going again depends on many factors, of course. Individual circumstances vary. No one widow's life will be just like another's.

Your preparation for your family's security will

Women in U.S. Labor Force

Percentage Projection to 1990

Percentage of Labor Force By Sex	1960	1972	1990
Men	67.9%	62.6%	61.2%
Women	32.1%	37.4%	38.8%

Source: U.S. Department of Labor

help ease the way for your widow. Anyone is bound to feel better about the world and her ability to handle things if she has been prepared. That preparation is a gift you are bestowing upon your wife by teaching her now how to be a widow.

Despite the hardships and heartaches of those days, weeks, and months while first on her own, she at least will not have to operate in bewilderment or panic because she does not understand her legal and financial situation or know what is possible for her future. She will know how you have organized your mutual affairs, and she will know to whom to turn for help. What's more, she will feel reasonably confident about her ability to take charge, for you will have established that confidence together.

Once the initial shock is over and the details of handling your estate are under way, your wife may be ready to take stock of her affairs in a more forward-looking light. She will have a good idea of what financial assets she will be able to rely on once probate is through. (Hopefully, your executor can be fairly precise about taxes and other such matters by this stage.)

Just as you and your wife sat down to figure what

U.S. Labor Force by Age Groups

Percentage Projection to 1990

Percentage of Labor Force By Age	1960	1972	1990
16-19	7.2%	9.4%	6.3%
20-34	31.3%	36.5%	38.9%
35-54	43.7%	37.9%	40.8%
55 and over	17.7%	16.3%	14.1%

Note: Percentages do not always add to 100 because of rounding.

Source: U.S. Department of Labor

you were worth when you first began to plan your estate, so she should now list her assets and debits and get a clear picture of where she stands. What is her net worth, once the estate is settled? What will she have to live on as steady income? What major expenditures, like college tuition, must she begin to prepare for now, even though they may not arise until some time in the future?

This is the stage at which to decide how life insurance proceeds will be distributed—if your widow has the choice. It is also the time for her to talk with your broker in case it seems advisable to invest some money either to provide income while preserving capital or for growth if the potential income won't be needed right away.

Your widow should take a fresh look at all property, too. Should a second home be used for rental to supplement the cash picture? Does she have to sell anything to meet immediate expenses? Is there a better route than selling, such as using the property for a collateral loan? Does she need two cars now? What should be done with your personal property?

More Adults Return to School

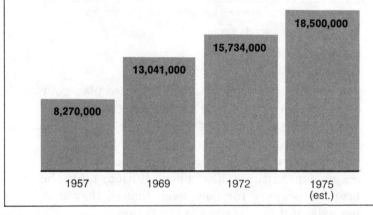

In 1957, 1 in every 13 people age 17 or above was enrolled part time in a formal adult-education activity. In 1975, nearly 1 in every 10 people was enrolled in an adult-education program, and, counting activities for which no enrollment was necessary, an estimated 1 in every 4 Americans undertook some form of adult education during the year.

Number of People Enrolled in Adult-Education Programs

Year	Enrolled
1957	8,270,000
1969	13,041,000
1972	15,734,000
1975 (est.)	18,500,000

Source: U.S. Office of Education

She should revise her will
It is also the time to revise her will to reflect the new situation. This should be done as carefully as you thought out your will and estate. If you have planned trust arrangements, your widow will want to review the plans with your banker or whomever else is trustee. Your insurance agent should be contacted, since it may be wise for your widow to take out more life insurance, perhaps including some declining term to cover the children's educational years. Property insurance policies should be changed in line with the different ownership. If your wife works to provide necessary income, she

should look into more health and disability income insurance, too.

Then, there may be difficult questions about the house. Can your wife afford to keep it up on her own, or will it no longer fit her budget? How important is remaining in familiar territory, weighed against problems she may confront with this specific house? Who will take care of maintenance? If you don't have teen-aged children, can your wife manage the lawn and plumbing? (No reason why she can't, if you have taught her about such things; or perhaps she was already taking care of such matters anyway.)

If your wife works, can she continue to work, while carrying other family burdens alone? Can she afford *not* to work? And if she does not now work, will she have to start? If so, how does she go about it? What kinds of jobs can she get?

Work possibilities for women are improving, although in one area traditionally thought of as "female"—teaching—there has been a scarcity of jobs in recent years. It would be foresight for your wife to refurbish her skills now, as you think together about the future. There are secretarial brush-up courses almost everywhere and retraining courses for other skills such as medical technicians and nurses. A part-time job to keep her hand in might even be enjoyable, preparing her to dig in full time, if necessary, either in a family financial crisis or later in widowhood.

That is not to say that all women must be secretaries or nurses. The point is that now is the time, while you are alive, for your wife to exercise her skills and emphasize her interests, with the idea of a job in mind for now or the future. By all means, encourage her to take courses at a nearby college,

Job Prospects: Good and Bad

Occupation	Projected 1980 Requirements	Percent Increase 1968 to 1980	Supply Estimated To Be
Chemists	200,000	55.7	
Counselors	107,000	49.8	
Dietitians	42,100	40.3	Significantly Below Requirements
Dentists	130,000	31.7	
Physicians	450,000	53.1	
Physicists	75,000	63.9	
Engineers	1,500,000	40.2	
Geologists & Geophysicists	36,000	20.6	Slightly Short of Requirements
Optometrists	21,000	23.5	
Architects	50,000	47.1	In Balance With Requirements
Lawyers	335,000	22.7	
Pharmacists	130,000	7.0	Slightly Above Requirements
Mathematicians	110,000	60.5	
Life Scientists	238,000	40.8	Significantly Above Requirements
Teachers, elementary and secondary	2,340,000	7.8	

Sources: U.S. Department of Labor, National Consumer Finance Association

if that is what she wants, or to get involved in volunteer work that interests her. Any dealings with the world outside your home can help strengthen her sense of self and provide experience that may become professionally useful.

It is important to talk over the work situation together now, for the question of working is often beset with emotional conflicts. Your wife may want very much to work and could feel comfortable doing so now; but she also may fear feeling guilty if she were away from the children when she would be the sole parent. Or she may just be terrified at the thought of working anywhere, whatever the circumstances.

These are feelings to be explored thoroughly. Often your discussion will do much to assuage fears, if only because your talking and planning together can point to practical solutions.

Your wife must think about what life style she would want if you were gone. Questions about selling the house without having you there to consult, or even taking a vacation when funds suddenly are limited, may overwhelm the unprepared widow. Better to explore them now, including the ticklish one of how you feel about your widow remarrying, or a stranger taking over as "father" in your house.

With all the planning, there still will be practical problems. For one thing, widows are prime targets for "con" men and outright crooks. Some of these dishonest persons watch the obituary pages to pick their newest prey. To crooks, widows seem likely to possess large sums along with little experience, so are fair game. And it is true that even the wisest and wealthiest of widows have lost portions of their inheritance by falling for some dishonest scheme. The more your wife learns now about the practical workings of money and family finance, the better she will be able to cope with the temptations "con" men offer.

Finally, your widow should look to her own needs and the possibilities for a full life ahead. She will have the confidence to solve her financial problems because her husband prepared her to deal with them on her own.

Appendix

Monthly Social Security Retirement Benefits

Note: These benefit figures are increased 6.4 percent effective June, 1976. The law provides for additional increases in benefits in future years, depending on increases in the cost of living.

Average Monthly Earnings	Worker Retiring At Age 65	Worker Retiring At Age 62
$ 0- 76	$101.40	$ 81.20
77- 78	103.00	82.40
79- 80	105.30	84.30
81- 81	107.30	85.90
82- 83	109.20	87.40
84- 85	111.50	89.20
86- 87	113.60	90.90
88- 89	115.40	92.40
90- 90	117.70	94.20
91- 92	119.70	95.80
93- 94	121.70	97.40
95- 96	123.60	98.90
97- 97	125.90	100.80
98- 99	128.00	102.40
100- 101	130.50	104.40
102- 102	132.30	105.90
103- 104	134.50	107.60
105- 106	137.00	109.60
107- 107	139.20	111.40
108- 109	141.40	113.20
110- 113	143.60	114.90
114- 118	145.60	116.50
119- 122	147.90	118.40
123- 127	150.10	120.10
128- 132	152.40	122.00
133- 136	154.50	123.60
137- 141	156.50	125.20
142- 146	158.90	127.20
147- 150	161.10	128.90
151- 155	163.10	130.50
156- 160	165.50	132.40
161- 164	167.60	134.10
165- 169	169.80	135.90

Monthly Social Security Retirement Benefits

Average Monthly Earnings	Worker Retiring At Age 65	Worker Retiring At Age 62
170- 174	172.00	137.60
175- 178	174.10	139.30
179- 183	176.50	141.20
184- 188	178.50	142.80
189- 193	180.90	144.80
194- 197	183.10	146.50
198- 202	185.20	148.20
203- 207	187.60	150.10
208- 211	189.80	151.90
212- 216	191.60	153.30
217- 221	194.00	155.20
222- 225	196.20	157.00
226- 230	198.60	158.90
231- 235	200.70	160.60
236- 239	203.20	162.60
240- 244	205.10	164.10
245- 249	207.10	165.70
250- 253	209.70	167.80
254- 258	211.80	169.50
259- 263	213.60	170.90
264- 267	216.20	173.00
268- 272	218.30	174.70
273- 277	220.60	176.50
278- 281	222.70	178.20
282- 286	224.90	180.00
287- 291	227.30	181.90
292- 295	229.20	183.40
296- 300	231.60	185.30
301- 305	233.80	187.10
306- 309	235.80	188.70
310- 314	238.20	190.60
315- 319	240.20	192.20
320- 323	242.30	193.90
324- 328	244.70	195.80
329- 333	246.80	197.50
334- 337	249.30	199.50
338- 342	251.10	200.90
343- 347	253.30	202.70
348- 351	255.80	204.70

Monthly Social Security Retirement Benefits

Average Monthly Earnings	Worker Retiring At Age 65	Worker Retiring At Age 62
352- 356	257.80	206.30
357- 361	260.20	208.20
362- 365	262.30	209.90
366- 370	264.30	211.50
371- 375	266.70	213.40
376- 379	268.90	215.20
380- 384	271.20	217.00
385- 389	273.20	218.60
390- 393	275.30	220.30
394- 398	277.70	222.20
399- 403	279.80	223.90
404- 407	282.30	225.90
408- 412	284.10	227.30
413- 417	286.10	228.90
418- 421	288.20	230.60
422- 426	290.50	232.40
427- 431	292.40	234.00
432- 436	294.20	235.40
437- 440	296.70	237.40
441- 445	298.50	238.80
446- 450	300.50	240.40
451- 454	302.80	242.30
455- 459	304.70	243.80
460- 464	306.80	245.50
465- 468	308.70	247.00
469- 473	311.10	248.90
474- 478	312.80	250.30
479- 482	314.90	252.00
483- 487	317.10	253.70
488- 492	319.10	255.30
493- 496	321.10	256.90
497- 501	323.40	258.80
502- 506	325.20	260.20
507- 510	327.30	261.90
511- 515	329.30	263.50
516- 520	331.50	265.20
521- 524	333.40	266.80
525- 529	335.50	268.40
530- 534	337.80	270.30

Monthly Social Security Retirement Benefits

Average Monthly Earnings	Worker Retiring At Age 65	Worker Retiring At Age 62
535- 538	339.60	271.70
539- 543	341.70	273.40
544- 548	343.90	275.20
549- 553	345.90	276.80
554- 556	347.90	278.40
557- 560	349.50	279.60
561- 563	351.50	281.20
564- 567	353.30	282.70
568- 570	355.20	284.20
571- 574	356.90	265.60
575- 577	358.80	267.10
578- 581	360.40	288.40
582- 584	362.40	290.00
585- 588	364.00	291.20
589- 591	366.10	292.90
592- 595	367.90	294.40
596- 598	369.70	295.80
599- 602	371.50	297.20
603- 605	373.30	298.70
606- 609	375.10	300.10
610- 612	377.00	301.60
613- 616	378.80	303.10
617- 620	380.60	304.50
621- 623	382.40	306.00
624- 627	384.20	307.40
628- 630	386.00	308.80
631- 634	387.80	310.30
635- 637	389.70	311.80
638- 641	391.70	313.40
642- 644	393.30	314.70
645- 648	395.20	316.20
649- 652	396.90	317.60
653- 656	398.10	318.50
657- 660	399.20	319.40
661- 665	400.60	320.50
666- 670	402.00	321.60
671- 675	403.50	322.80
676- 680	404.90	324.00
681- 685	406.30	325.10

Monthly Social Security Retirement Benefits

Average Monthly Earnings	Worker Retiring At Age 65	Worker Retiring At Age 62
686- 690	407.90	326.40
691- 695	409.30	327.50
696- 700	410.70	328.60
701- 705	412.20	329.80
706- 710	413.60	330.90
711- 715	415.00	332.00
716- 720	416.50	333.20
721- 725	417.90	334.40
726- 730	419.30	335.50
731- 735	420.70	336.60
736- 740	422.20	337.80
741- 745	423.60	338.90
746- 750	425.00	340.00
751- 755	426.30	341.10
756- 760	427.50	342.00
761- 765	428.70	343.00
766- 770	429.90	344.00
771- 775	431.10	344.90
776- 780	432.30	345.90
781- 785	433.50	346.80
786- 790	434.60	347.70
791- 795	435.80	348.70
796- 800	437.00	349.60
801- 805	438.30	350.70
806- 810	439.50	351.60
811- 815	440.70	352.60
816- 820	441.90	353.60
821- 825	443.10	354.50
826- 830	444.30	355.50
831- 835	445.40	356.40
836- 840	446.60	357.30
841- 845	447.80	358.30
846- 850	449.00	359.20
851- 855	450.30	360.30
856- 860	451.50	361.20
861- 865	452.70	362.20
866- 870	453.90	363.20
871- 875	455.10	364.10
876- 880	456.20	365.00

Monthly Social Security Retirement Benefits

Average Monthly Earnings	Worker Retiring At Age 65	Worker Retiring At Age 62
881- 885	457.40	366.00
886- 890	458.60	366.90
891- 895	459.80	367.90
896- 900	461.00	368.80
901- 905	462.30	369.90
906- 910	463.50	370.80
911- 915	464.70	371.80
916- 920	465.90	372.80
921- 925	467.00	373.60
926- 930	468.20	374.60
931- 935	469.40	375.60
936- 940	470.60	376.50
941- 945	471.80	377.50
946- 950	473.00	378.40
951- 955	474.30	379.50
956- 960	475.50	380.40
961- 965	476.70	381.40
966- 970	477.80	382.30
971- 975	479.00	383.20
976- 980	480.20	384.20
981- 985	481.40	385.20
986- 990	482.60	386.10
991- 995	483.80	387.10
996-1,000	485.00	388.00
1,001-1,005	486.00	388.80
1,006-1,010	487.10	389.70
1,011-1,015	488.20	390.60
1,016-1,020	489.30	391.50
1,021-1,025	490.40	392.40
1,026-1,030	491.40	393.20
1,031-1,035	492.50	394.00
1,036-1,040	493.60	394.90
1,041-1,045	494.70	395.80
1,046-1,050	495.80	396.70
1,051-1,055	496.80	397.50
1,056-1,060	497.90	398.40
1,061-1,065	499.00	399.20
1,066-1,070	500.10	400.10
1,071-1,075	501.20	401.00

Monthly Social Security Retirement Benefits

Average Monthly Earnings	Worker Retiring At Age 65	Worker Retiring At Age 62
1,076-1,080	502.20	401.80
1,081-1,085	503.30	402.70
1,086-1,090	504.40	403.60
1,091-1,095	505.50	404.40
1,096-1,100	506.60	405.30
1,101-1,105	507.60	406.10
1,106-1,110	508.70	407.00
1,111-1,115	509.80	407.90
1,116-1,120	510.90	408.80
1,121-1,125	512.00	409.60
1,126-1,130	513.00	410.40
1,131-1,135	514.10	411.30
1,136-1,140	515.20	412.20
1,141-1,145	516.30	413.10
1,146-1,150	517.40	414.00
1,151-1,155	518.40	414.80
1,156-1,160	519.50	415.60
1,161-1,165	520.60	416.50
1,166-1,170	521.70	417.40
1,171-1,175	522.80	418.30

Monthly Social Security Benefits for Survivors

Note: These benefit figures are increased 6.4 percent effective June, 1976. The law provides for additional increases in benefits in future years, depending on increases in the cost of living.

Average Monthly Earnings		Widow or Widower Claiming Benefit			One Child	Mother and		Maximum Family Benefit
		Age 65 Or Over	Age 60	Age 50		One Child	Two Children	
$ 0-	76	$101.40	$ 74.90	$ 56.80	$101.40	$152.20	$152.10	$152.10
77-	78	103.00	74.90	56.80	101.40	154.60	154.50	154.50
79-	80	105.30	75.30	56.80	101.40	158.00	158.10	158.10
81-	81	107.30	76.80	56.80	101.40	161.00	161.10	161.00
82-	83	109.20	78.10	56.80	101.40	163.80	164.10	163.90
84-	85	111.50	79.80	56.80	101.40	167.40	167.40	167.30
86-	87	113.60	81.30	56.90	101.40	170.40	170.40	170.40
88-	89	115.40	82.60	57.80	101.40	173.20	173.10	173.10
90-	90	117.70	84.20	58.90	101.40	176.60	176.70	176.60
91-	92	119.70	85.60	59.90	101.40	179.60	179.70	179.60
93-	94	121.70	87.10	61.00	101.40	182.60	182.70	182.60
95-	96	123.60	88.40	61.90	101.40	185.40	185.40	185.40
97-	97	125.90	90.10	63.10	101.40	189.00	189.00	188.90
98-	99	128.00	91.60	64.10	101.40	192.00	192.30	192.10
100-	101	130.50	93.40	65.40	101.40	195.80	195.90	195.80
102-	102	132.30	94.60	66.20	101.40	198.40	198.60	198.60
103-	104	134.50	96.20	67.30	101.40	201.80	201.90	201.80
105-	106	137.00	98.00	68.60	102.80	205.60	205.50	205.50
107-	107	139.20	99.60	69.70	104.40	208.80	208.80	208.80
108-	109	141.40	101.20	70.80	106.10	212.20	212.40	212.20
110-	113	143.60	102.70	71.90	107.70	215.40	215.40	215.40
114-	118	145.60	104.20	72.90	109.20	218.40	218.40	218.40
119-	122	147.90	105.80	74.10	111.00	222.00	222.00	221.90
123-	127	150.10	107.40	75.20	112.60	225.20	225.30	225.20
128-	132	152.40	109.00	76.30	114.30	228.60	228.90	228.70
133-	136	154.50	110.50	77.30	115.90	231.80	231.90	231.80
137-	141	156.50	111.90	78.30	117.40	234.80	234.90	234.80
142-	146	158.90	113.70	79.60	119.20	238.40	238.50	238.40
147-	150	161.10	115.20	80.60	120.90	241.80	241.80	241.70
151-	155	163.10	116.70	81.70	122.40	244.80	244.80	244.70
156-	160	165.50	118.40	82.90	124.20	248.40	248.40	248.30
161-	164	167.60	119.90	83.90	125.70	251.40	251.40	251.40
165-	169	169.80	121.50	85.00	127.40	254.80	254.70	254.70

Monthly Social Security Benefits for Survivors

Average Monthly Earnings	Widow or Widower Claiming Benefit			One Child	Mother and		Maximum Family Benefit
	Age 65 Or Over	Age 60	Age 50		One Child	Two Children	
170- 174	172.00	123.00	86.10	129.00	258.00	258.30	258.10
175- 178	174.10	124.50	87.10	130.60	261.20	261.30	261.20
179- 183	176.50	126.20	88.30	132.40	264.80	264.90	264.80
184- 188	178.50	127.70	89.40	133.90	267.80	267.90	267.80
189- 193	180.90	129.40	90.60	135.70	271.40	271.80	271.60
194- 197	183.10	131.00	91.70	137.40	274.80	274.80	274.80
198- 202	185.20	132.50	92.70	138.90	277.80	277.80	277.80
203- 207	187.60	134.20	93.90	140.70	281.40	281.70	281.50
208- 211	189.80	135.80	95.00	142.40	284.80	284.70	284.70
212- 216	191.60	137.00	95.90	143.70	287.40	287.40	287.40
217- 221	194.00	138.80	97.10	145.50	291.00	291.00	291.00
222- 225	196.20	140.30	98.20	147.20	294.40	294.30	294.30
226- 230	190.60	142.00	99.40	149.00	298.00	297.90	297.90
231- 235	200.70	143.60	100.50	150.60	301.20	301.20	301.10
236- 239	203.20	145.30	101.70	152.40	304.80	304.80	304.80
240- 244	205.10	146.70	102.70	153.90	307.80	309.30	309.10
245- 249	207.10	148.10	103.60	155.40	310.80	315.60	315.50
250- 253	209.70	150.00	105.00	157.30	314.60	320.70	320.60
254- 258	211.80	151.50	106.00	158.90	317.80	327.00	326.90
259- 263	213.60	152.80	106.90	160.20	320.40	333.30	333.10
264- 267	216.20	154.60	108.20	162.20	324.40	338.40	338.20
268- 272	218.30	156.10	109.20	163.80	327.60	344.70	344.60
273- 277	220.60	157.80	110.40	165.50	331.00	351.00	350.80
278- 281	222.70	159.30	111.50	167.10	334.20	356.10	355.90
282- 286	224.90	160.90	112.60	168.70	337.40	362.40	362.30
287- 291	227.30	162.60	113.80	170.50	341.00	368.70	368.70
292- 295	229.20	163.90	114.70	171.90	343.80	373.80	373.60
296- 300	231.60	165.60	115.90	173.70	347.40	380.10	379.90
301- 305	233.80	167.20	117.00	175.40	350.80	386.40	386.30
306- 309	235.80	168.60	118.00	176.90	353.80	391.50	391.40
310- 314	238.20	170.40	119.20	178.70	357.40	397.80	397.70
315- 319	240.20	171.80	120.20	180.20	360.40	404.10	404.10
320- 323	242.30	173.30	121.30	181.60	363.60	409.20	409.20
324- 328	244.70	175.00	122.40	183.60	367.20	415.50	415.50
329- 333	246.80	176.50	123.50	185.10	370.20	421.80	421.80
334- 337	249.30	178.30	124.80	187.00	374.00	426.90	426.90

Monthly Social Security Benefits for Survivors

Average Monthly Earnings	Widow or Widower Claiming Benefit			One Child	Mother and		Maximum Family Benefit
	Age 65 Or Over	Age 60	Age 50		One Child	Two Children	
338- 342	251.10	179.60	125.70	188.40	376.80	433.20	433.10
343- 347	253.30	181.20	126.80	190.00	380.00	439.50	439.50
348- 351	255.80	182.90	128.00	191.90	383.80	444.60	444.50
352- 356	257.80	184.40	129.00	193.40	386.80	450.90	450.80
357- 361	260.20	186.10	130.20	195.20	390.40	457.20	457.20
362- 365	262.30	187.60	131.30	196.80	393.60	462.30	462.30
366- 370	264.30	189.00	132.20	198.30	396.60	468.60	468.60
371- 375	266.70	190.70	133.40	200.10	400.20	474.90	474.80
376- 379	268.90	192.30	134.50	201.70	403.40	480.30	480.10
380- 384	271.20	194.00	135.70	203.40	406.80	486.60	486.40
385- 389	273.20	195.40	136.70	204.90	409.80	492.60	492.60
390- 393	275.30	196.90	137.80	206.50	413.00	497.70	497.70
394- 398	277.70	198.60	138.90	208.30	416.60	504.30	504.10
399- 403	279.80	200.10	140.00	209.90	419.80	510.60	510.50
404- 407	282.30	201.90	141.30	211.80	423.60	515.40	515.40
408- 412	284.10	203.20	142.20	213.10	426.20	522.00	521.80
413- 417	286.10	204.60	143.10	214.60	429.20	528.30	528.10
418- 421	286.20	206.10	144.20	216.20	432.40	533.10	533.10
422- 426	290.50	207.80	145.40	217.90	435.80	539.40	539.40
427- 431	292.40	209.10	146.30	219.30	438.60	546.00	545.80
432- 436	294.20	210.40	147.20	220.70	441.40	552.30	552.10
437- 440	296.70	212.20	148.50	222.60	445.20	554.70	554.60
441- 445	298.50	213.50	149.40	223.90	447.80	558.00	557.90
446- 450	300.50	214.90	150.30	225.40	450.80	561.00	561.00
451- 454	302.80	216.60	151.50	227.10	454.20	563.70	563.50
455- 459	304.70	217.90	152.40	228.60	457.20	566.70	566.60
460- 464	306.60	219.40	153.50	230.10	460.20	569.70	569.70
465- 468	308.70	220.80	154.50	231.60	463.20	572.40	572.40
469- 473	311.10	222.50	155.70	233.40	466.80	575.70	575.50
474- 478	312.80	223.70	156.50	234.60	469.20	578.70	578.70
479- 482	314.90	225.20	157.50	236.20	472.40	581.40	581.30
483- 487	317.10	226.80	158.70	237.90	475.80	584.70	584.50
488- 492	319.10	228.20	159.60	239.40	478.80	587.70	587.70
493- 496	321.10	229.60	160.60	240.90	481.80	590.40	590.20
497- 501	323.40	231.30	161.80	242.60	485.20	593.40	593.30
502- 506	325.20	232.60	162.70	243.90	487.80	596.40	596.40

Monthly Social Security Benefits for Survivors

Average Monthly Earnings	Widow or Widower Claiming Benefit			One Child	Mother and		Maximum Family Benefit
	Age 65 Or Over	Age 60	Age 50		One Child	Two Children	
507- 510	327.30	234.10	163.90	245.50	491.00	599.10	599.00
511- 515	329.30	235.50	164.80	247.00	494.00	602.10	602.10
516- 520	331.50	237.10	165.90	248.70	497.40	605.40	605.40
521- 524	333.40	238.40	166.80	250.10	500.20	607.80	607.80
525- 529	335.50	239.90	167.80	251.70	503.40	611.10	611.00
530- 534	337.80	241.60	169.00	253.40	506.80	614.10	614.10
535- 538	339.60	242.90	169.90	254.70	509.40	616.80	616.70
539- 543	341.70	244.40	171.00	256.30	512.60	620.10	619.90
544- 548	343.90	245.90	172.00	258.00	516.00	623.10	623.00
549- 553	345.90	247.40	173.10	259.50	519.00	626.40	626.20
554- 556	347.90	248.80	174.10	261.00	522.00	628.20	628.10
557- 560	349.50	249.90	174.80	262.20	524.40	630.90	630.70
561- 563	351.50	251.40	175.90	263.70	527.40	632.70	632.60
564- 567	353.30	252.70	176.80	265.00	530.00	635.10	635.10
568- 570	355.20	254.00	177.70	266.40	532.80	637.20	637.00
571- 574	356.90	255.20	178.50	267.70	535.40	639.60	639.40
575- 577	358.80	256.60	179.50	269.10	538.20	641.70	641.50
578- 581	360.40	257.70	180.30	270.30	540.60	643.80	643.80
582- 584	362.40	259.20	181.30	271.80	543.60	645.90	645.80
585- 588	364.00	260.30	182.10	273.00	546.00	648.60	648.40
589- 591	366.10	261.80	183.10	274.60	549.20	650.40	650.20
592- 595	367.90	263.10	184.10	276.00	552.00	652.80	652.80
596- 598	369.70	264.40	185.00	277.30	554.60	654.60	654.60
599- 602	371.50	265.70	185.90	278.70	557.40	657.30	657.30
603- 605	373.30	267.00	186.80	280.00	560.00	659.40	659.20
606- 609	375.10	268.20	187.60	281.40	562.80	661.50	661.50
610- 612	377.00	269.60	188.60	282.80	565.60	663.60	663.60
613- 616	378.80	270.90	189.50	284.10	568.20	666.30	666.10
617- 620	380.60	272.20	190.40	285.50	571.00	668.70	668.70
621- 623	382.40	273.50	191.30	286.80	573.60	670.50	670.50
624- 627	384.20	274.80	192.20	288.20	576.40	673.20	673.10
628- 630	386.00	276.00	193.10	289.50	579.00	675.60	675.40
631- 634	387.80	277.30	194.00	290.90	581.80	678.90	678.70
635- 637	389.70	278.70	195.00	292.30	584.60	681.90	681.90
638- 641	391.70	280.10	195.90	293.80	587.60	685.20	685.20
642- 644	393.30	281.30	196.80	295.00	590.00	688.20	688.20

Monthly Social Security Benefits for Survivors

Average Monthly Earnings	Widow or Widower Claiming Benefit Age 65 Or Over	Age 60	Age 50	One Child	Mother and One Child	Two Children	Maximum Family Benefit
645- 648	395.20	282.60	197.70	296.40	592.80	691.80	691.60
649- 652	396.90	283.80	198.50	297.70	595.40	694.80	694.60
653- 656	398.10	284.70	199.20	298.60	597.20	696.60	696.60
657- 660	399.20	285.50	199.70	299.40	598.80	698.70	698.50
661- 665	400.60	286.50	200.40	300.50	601.00	701.10	701.10
666- 670	402.00	287.50	201.10	301.50	603.00	703.80	703.60
671- 675	403.50	288.60	201.90	302.70	605.40	706.20	706.00
676- 680	404.90	289.60	202.60	303.70	607.40	708.60	708.60
681- 685	406.30	290.60	203.30	304.80	609.60	711.30	711.10
686- 690	407.90	291.70	204.10	306.00	612.00	713.70	713.60
691- 695	409.30	292.70	204.80	307.00	614.00	716.40	716.20
696- 700	410.70	293.70	205.40	308.10	616.20	718.80	718.70
701- 705	412.20	294.80	206.20	309.20	618.40	721.20	721.20
706- 710	413.60	295.80	206.90	310.20	620.40	723.60	723.60
711- 715	415.00	296.80	207.60	311.30	622.60	726.30	726.20
716- 720	416.50	297.80	208.30	312.40	624.80	728.70	728.70
721- 725	417.90	298.80	209.00	313.50	627.00	731.40	731.20
726- 730	419.30	299.80	209.70	314.50	629.00	733.80	733.80
731- 735	420.70	300.90	210.50	315.60	631.20	736.50	736.30
736- 740	422.20	301.90	211.20	316.70	633.40	738.90	738.80
741- 745	423.60	302.90	211.90	317.70	635.40	741.60	741.40
746- 750	425.00	303.90	212.60	318.80	637.60	744.00	743.80
751- 755	426.30	304.90	213.30	319.80	639.60	746.10	746.00
756- 760	427.50	305.70	213.80	320.70	641.40	748.20	748.10
761- 765	428.70	306.60	214.50	321.60	643.20	750.30	750.20
766- 770	429.90	307.40	215.00	322.50	645.00	752.40	752.30
771- 775	431.10	308.30	215.70	323.40	646.80	754.50	754.40
776- 780	432.30	309.10	216.20	324.30	648.60	756.60	756.40
781- 785	433.50	310.00	216.80	325.20	650.40	758.70	758.50
786- 790	434.60	310.80	217.40	326.00	652.00	760.80	760.60
791- 795	435.80	311.60	218.00	326.90	653.80	762.90	762.70
796- 800	437.00	312.50	218.60	327.80	655.60	765.00	764.80
801- 805	438.30	313.40	219.20	328.80	657.60	767.10	767.00
806- 810	439.50	314.30	219.90	329.70	659.40	769.20	769.00
811- 815	440.70	315.20	220.50	330.60	661.20	771.30	771.20
816- 820	441.90	316.00	221.00	331.50	663.00	773.40	773.20

Monthly Social Security Benefits for Survivors

Average Monthly Earnings	Widow or Widower Claiming Benefit Age 65 Or Over	Age 60	Age 50	One Child	Mother and One Child	Two Children	Maximum Family Benefit
821- 825	443.10	316.90	221.70	332.40	664.80	775.50	775.40
826- 830	444.30	317.70	222.20	333.30	666.60	777.60	777.40
831- 835	445.40	318.50	222.80	334.10	668.20	779.70	779.60
836- 840	446.60	319.40	223.40	335.00	670.00	781.80	781.60
841- 845	447.80	320.20	224.00	335.90	671.80	783.90	783.80
846- 850	449.00	321.10	224.60	336.80	673.60	785.70	785.70
851- 855	450.30	322.00	225.20	337.80	675.60	788.10	787.90
856- 860	451.50	322.90	225.90	338.70	677.40	790.20	790.00
861- 865	452.70	323.70	226.40	339.60	679.20	792.30	792.10
866- 870	453.90	324.60	227.10	340.50	681.00	794.40	794.20
871- 875	455.10	325.40	227.60	341.40	682.80	796.50	796.30
876- 880	456.20	326.20	228.20	342.20	684.40	798.60	798.40
881- 885	457.40	327.10	228.80	343.10	686.20	800.70	800.50
886- 890	458.60	327.90	229.40	344.00	688.00	802.80	802.60
891- 895	459.80	328.80	230.00	344.90	689.80	804.90	804.80
896- 900	461.00	329.70	230.60	345.80	691.60	807.00	806.80
901- 905	462.30	330.60	231.30	346.80	693.60	809.10	809.00
906- 910	463.50	331.50	231.90	347.70	695.40	811.20	811.00
911- 915	464.70	332.30	232.40	348.60	697.20	813.30	813.20
916- 920	465.90	333.20	233.10	349.50	699.00	815.10	815.10
921- 925	467.00	334.00	233.60	350.30	700.60	817.50	817.30
926- 930	468.20	334.80	234.20	351.20	702.40	819.30	819.30
931- 935	469.40	335.70	234.80	352.10	704.20	821.70	821.50
936- 940	470.60	336.50	235.40	353.00	706.00	823.50	823.50
941- 945	471.80	337.40	236.00	353.90	707.80	825.90	825.70
946- 950	473.00	338.20	236.60	354.80	709.60	828.00	827.80
951- 955	474.30	339.20	237.30	355.80	711.60	830.10	829.90
956- 960	475.50	340.00	237.80	356.70	713.40	832.20	832.00
961- 965	476.70	340.90	238.50	357.60	715.20	834.30	834.10
966- 970	477.80	341.70	239.00	358.40	716.80	836.40	836.20
971- 975	479.00	342.50	239.60	359.30	718.60	838.50	838.30
976- 980	480.20	343.40	240.20	360.20	720.40	840.30	840.30
981- 985	481.40	344.30	240.80	361.10	722.20	842.40	842.40
986- 990	482.60	345.10	241.40	362.00	724.00	844.50	844.50
991- 995	483.80	346.00	242.00	362.90	725.80	846.90	846.70
996-1,000	485.00	346.80	242.60	363.60	727.60	848.70	848.70

Monthly Social Security Benefits for Survivors

Average Monthly Earnings	Widow or Widower Claiming Benefit Age 65 Or Over	Age 60	Age 50	One Child	Mother and One Child	Two Children	Maximum Family Benefit
1,001-1,005	486.00	347.50	243.10	364.50	729.00	850.50	850.50
1,006-1,010	487.10	348.30	243.60	365.40	730.80	852.60	852.50
1,011-1,015	488.20	349.10	244.20	366.20	732.40	854.40	854.30
1,016-1,020	489.30	349.90	244.80	367.00	734.00	856.50	856.30
1,021-1,025	490.40	350.70	245.30	367.80	735.60	858.30	858.10
1,026-1,030	491.40	351.40	245.80	368.60	737.20	860.10	860.10
1,031-1,035	492.50	352.20	246.40	369.40	738.80	861.90	861.90
1,036-1,040	493.60	353.00	246.90	370.20	740.40	864.00	863.80
1,041-1,045	494.70	353.80	247.50	371.10	742.20	865.80	865.70
1,046-1,050	495.80	354.50	248.00	371.90	743.80	867.60	867.60
1,051-1,055	496.80	355.30	248.50	372.60	745.20	869.40	869.40
1,056-1,060	497.90	356.00	249.00	373.50	747.00	871.50	871.40
1,061-1,065	499.00	356.80	249.60	374.30	748.60	873.30	873.20
1,066-1,070	500.10	357.60	250.10	375.10	750.20	875.40	875.20
1,071-1,075	501.20	358.40	250.70	375.90	751.80	877.20	877.00
1,076-1,080	502.20	359.10	251.20	376.70	753.40	879.00	879.00
1,081-1,085	503.30	359.90	251.70	377.50	755.00	880.80	880.80
1,086-1,090	504.40	360.70	252.30	378.30	756.60	882.90	882.70
1,091-1,095	505.50	361.50	252.90	379.20	758.40	884.70	884.60
1,096-1,100	506.60	362.30	253.40	380.00	760.00	886.50	886.50
1,101-1,105	507.60	363.00	253.90	380.70	761.40	888.30	888.30
1,106-1,110	508.70	363.80	254.50	381.60	763.20	890.40	890.30
1,111-1,115	509.80	364.60	255.00	382.40	764.80	892.20	892.10
1,116-1,120	510.90	365.30	255.50	383.20	766.40	894.30	894.10
1,121-1,125	512.00	366.10	256.10	384.00	768.00	896.10	895.90
1,126-1,130	513.00	366.80	256.60	384.80	769.60	897.90	897.90
1,131-1,135	514.10	367.60	257.10	385.60	771.20	899.70	899.70
1,136-1,140	515.20	368.40	257.70	386.40	772.80	901.80	901.60
1,141-1,145	516.30	369.20	258.20	387.30	774.60	903.60	903.50
1,146-1,150	517.40	370.00	258.80	388.10	776.20	905.40	905.40
1,151-1,155	518.40	370.70	259.30	388.80	777.60	907.20	907.20
1,156-1,160	519.50	371.50	259.90	389.70	779.40	909.30	909.20
1,161-1,165	520.60	372.30	260.40	390.50	781.00	911.10	911.00
1,166-1,170	521.70	373.10	261.00	391.30	782.60	913.20	913.00
1,171-1,175	522.80	373.90	261.50	392.10	784.20	915.00	914.80

Monthly Social Security Retirement Benefits For Worker With Spouse

Note: These benefit figures are increased 6.4 percent effective June, 1976. The law provides for additional increases in benefits in future years, depending on increases in the cost of living.

Average Monthly Earnings		Worker Retiring at Age 65 With Spouse		
		Age 65 Or Over	Age 62	With Spouse & One Child
$ 0-	76	$152.10	$139.50	$152.20
77-	78	154.50	141.70	154.60
79-	80	158.00	144.90	158.10
81-	81	161.00	147.60	161.10
82-	83	163.80	150.20	164.00
84-	85	167.30	153.40	167.30
86-	87	170.40	156.20	170.40
88-	89	173.10	158.70	173.20
90-	90	176.60	161.90	176.70
91-	92	179.60	164.70	179.70
93-	94	182.60	167.40	182.70
95-	96	185.40	170.00	185.40
97-	97	188.90	173.20	188.90
98-	99	192.00	176.00	192.20
100-	101	195.80	179.50	195.90
102-	102	198.50	182.00	198.70
103-	104	201.80	185.00	201.90
105-	106	205.50	188.40	205.60
107-	107	208.80	191.40	208.80
108-	109	212.10	194.50	212.20
110-	113	215.40	197.50	215.40
114-	118	218.40	200.20	218.40
119-	122	221.90	203.40	221.90
123-	127	225.20	206.50	225.30
128-	132	228.60	209.60	228.80
133-	136	231.80	212.50	231.90
137-	141	234.80	215.30	234.90
142-	146	238.40	218.60	238.50
147-	150	241.70	221.60	241.70
151-	155	244.70	224.30	244.70
156-	160	248.30	227.60	248.30
161-	164	251.40	230.50	251.40
165-	169	254.70	233.50	254.80

Monthly Social Security Retirement Benefits For Worker With Spouse

Average Monthly Earnings	Worker Retiring at Age 65 With Spouse		
	Age 65 Or Over	Age 62	With Spouse & One Child
170- 174	258.00	236.50	258.20
175- 178	261.20	239.50	261.30
179- 183	264.80	242.80	264.90
184- 188	267.80	245.50	267.90
189- 193	271.40	248.80	271.70
194- 197	274.70	251.80	274.90
198- 202	277.80	254.70	277.80
203- 207	281.40	258.00	281.60
208- 211	284.70	261.00	284.80
212- 216	287.40	263.50	287.40
217- 221	291.00	266.80	291.00
222- 225	294.30	269.80	294.40
226- 230	297.90	273.10	298.00
231- 235	301.10	276.00	301.10
236- 239	304.80	279.40	304.60
240- 244	307.70	282.10	309.10
245- 249	310.70	284.80	315.50
250- 253	314.60	288.40	320.70
254- 258	317.70	291.30	327.00
259- 263	320.40	293.70	333.20
264- 267	324.30	297.30	338.20
268- 272	327.50	300.20	344.70
273- 277	330.90	303.40	350.80
278- 281	334.10	306.30	355.90
282- 286	337.40	309.30	362.30
287- 291	341.00	312.60	368.70
292- 295	343.80	315.20	373.60
296- 300	347.40	318.50	380.00
301- 305	350.70	321.50	386.40
306- 309	353.70	324.30	391.40
310- 314	357.30	327.60	397.80
315- 319	360.30	330.30	404.20
320- 323	363.50	333.20	409.30
324- 328	367.10	336.50	415.50
329- 333	370.20	339.40	421.80
334- 337	374.00	342.90	426.90

Monthly Social Security Retirement Benefits For Worker With Spouse

| Average Monthly Earnings | Worker Retiring at Age 65 With Spouse | | |
	Age 65 Or Over	Age 62	With Spouse & One Child
338- 342	376.70	345.30	433.10
343- 347	380.00	348.40	439.50
348- 351	383.70	351.80	444.60
352- 356	386.70	354.50	450.80
357- 361	390.30	357.80	457.20
362- 365	393.50	360.70	462.30
366- 370	396.50	363.50	468.70
371- 375	400.10	366.80	474.90
376- 379	403.40	369.80	480.10
380- 384	406.80	372.90	486.40
385- 389	409.80	375.70	492.60
390- 393	413.00	378.60	497.70
394- 398	416.60	381.90	504.10
399- 403	419.70	384.80	510.60
404- 407	423.50	388.20	515.50
408- 412	426.20	390.70	521.90
413- 417	429.20	393.50	528.10
418- 421	432.30	396.30	533.20
422- 426	435.80	399.50	539.50
427- 431	438.60	402.10	545.80
432- 436	441.30	404.60	552.20
437- 440	445.10	408.00	554.70
441- 445	447.80	410.50	557.90
446- 450	450.80	413.30	561.10
451- 454	454.20	416.40	563.60
455- 459	457.10	419.00	566.70
460- 464	460.20	421.90	569.80
465- 468	463.10	424.50	572.50
469- 473	466.70	427.80	575.50
474- 478	469.20	430.10	578.80
479- 482	472.40	433.10	581.30
483- 487	475.70	436.10	584.50
488- 492	478.70	438.80	587.70
493- 496	481.70	441.60	590.30
497- 501	485.10	444.70	593.40
502- 506	487.80	447.20	596.40

Monthly Social Security Retirement Benefits For Worker With Spouse

| Average Monthly Earnings | Worker Retiring at Age 65 With Spouse | | With Spouse & One Child |
	Age 65 Or Over	Age 62	
507- 510	491.00	450.10	599.10
511- 515	494.00	452.90	602.10
516- 520	497.30	455.90	605.50
521- 524	500.10	458.50	607.80
525- 529	503.30	461.40	611.10
530- 534	506.70	464.50	614.20
535- 538	509.40	467.00	616.80
539- 543	512.60	469.90	619.90
544- 548	515.90	472.90	623.10
549- 553	518.90	475.70	626.30
554- 556	521.90	478.40	628.10
557- 560	524.30	480.60	630.70
561- 563	527.30	483.40	632.70
564- 567	530.00	485.90	635.10
568- 570	532.80	488.40	637.00
571- 574	535.40	490.80	639.50
575- 577	538.20	493.40	641.60
578- 581	540.60	495.60	643.80
582- 584	543.60	498.30	645.00
585- 588	546.00	500.50	648.40
589- 591	549.20	503.50	650.30
592- 595	551.90	505.90	652.90
596- 598	554.60	508.40	654.70
599- 602	557.30	510.90	657.30
603- 605	560.00	513.40	659.30
606- 609	562.70	515.80	661.50
610- 612	565.50	518.40	663.60
613- 616	568.20	520.90	666.20
617- 620	570.90	523.40	668.80
621- 623	573.60	525.80	670.60
624- 627	576.30	528.30	673.20
628- 630	579.00	530.80	675.40
631- 634	581.70	533.30	678.80
635- 637	584.60	535.90	681.90
638- 641	587.60	538.70	685.30
642- 644	590.00	540.90	688.30

Monthly Social Security Retirement Benefits
For Worker With Spouse

| Average Monthly Earnings | Worker Retiring at Age 65 With Spouse | | With Spouse & One Child |
	Age 65 Or Over	Age 62	
645- 648	592.80	543.40	691.60
649- 652	595.40	545.80	694.70
653- 656	597.20	547.50	696.70
657- 660	598.80	548.90	698.60
661- 665	600.90	550.90	701.20
666- 670	603.00	552.80	703.60
671- 675	605.30	554.90	708.10
676- 680	607.40	556.80	708.70
681- 685	609.50	558.70	711.10
686- 690	611.90	560.90	713.70
691- 695	614.00	562.90	716.30
696- 700	616.10	564.80	718.70
701- 705	618.30	566.80	721.20
706- 710	620.40	568.70	723.60
711- 715	622.50	570.70	726.20
716- 720	624.80	572.80	728.70
721- 725	626.90	574.70	731.30
726- 730	629.00	576.60	733.90
731- 735	631.10	578.50	736.30
736- 740	633.30	580.60	738.80
741- 745	635.40	582.50	741.40
746- 750	637.50	584.40	743.80
751- 755	639.50	586.20	746.10
756- 760	641.30	587.90	748.10
761- 765	643.10	589.50	750.30
766- 770	644.90	591.20	752.30
771- 775	646.70	592.80	754.50
776- 780	648.50	594.50	756.50
781- 785	650.30	596.10	758.50
786- 790	651.90	597.60	760.60
791- 795	653.70	599.30	762.80
796- 800	655.50	600.90	764.80
801- 805	657.50	602.70	767.10
806- 810	659.30	604.40	769.10
811- 815	661.10	606.00	771.30
816- 820	662.90	607.70	773.30

Monthly Social Security Retirement Benefits For Worker With Spouse

Average Monthly Earnings	Worker Retiring at Age 65 With Spouse Age 65 Or Over	Age 62	With Spouse & One Child
821- 825	664.70	609.30	775.50
826- 830	666.50	611.00	777.50
831- 835	668.10	612.50	779.60
836- 840	669.90	614.10	781.60
841- 845	671.70	615.80	783.80
846- 850	673.50	617.40	785.80
851- 855	675.50	619.20	787.90
856- 860	677.30	620.90	790.10
861- 865	679.10	622.50	792.10
866- 870	680.90	624.20	794.30
871- 875	682.70	625.80	796.30
876- 880	684.30	627.30	798.40
881- 885	686.10	629.00	800.60
886- 890	687.90	630.60	802.60
891- 895	689.70	632.30	804.80
896- 900	691.50	633.90	806.80
901- 905	693.50	635.70	809.10
906- 910	695.30	637.40	811.10
911- 915	697.10	639.00	813.30
916- 920	698.90	640.70	815.10
921- 925	700.50	642.20	817.40
926- 930	702.30	643.80	819.40
931- 935	704.10	645.50	821.60
936- 940	705.90	647.10	823.60
941- 945	707.70	648.80	825.80
946- 950	709.50	650.40	827.80
951- 955	711.50	652.20	829.90
956- 960	713.30	653.90	832.10
961- 965	715.10	655.50	834.10
966- 970	716.70	657.00	836.20
971- 975	718.50	658.70	838.40
976- 980	720.30	660.30	840.40
981- 985	722.10	662.00	842.40
986- 990	723.90	663.60	844.60
991- 995	725.70	665.30	846.80
996-1,000	727.50	666.90	848.80

Monthly Social Security Retirement Benefits
For Worker With Spouse

Average Monthly Earnings	Worker Retiring at Age 65 With Spouse Age 65 Or Over	Age 62	With Spouse & One Child
1,001-1,005	729.00	668.30	850.60
1,006-1,010	730.70	669.80	852.50
1,011-1,015	732.30	671.30	854.40
1,016-1,020	734.00	672.90	856.30
1,021-1,025	735.60	674.30	858.20
1,026-1,030	737.10	675.70	860.20
1,031-1,035	738.80	677.30	861.90
1,036-1,040	740.40	678.70	863.80
1,041-1,045	742.10	680.30	865.70
1,046-1,050	743.70	681.80	867.60
1,051-1,055	745.20	683.10	869.40
1,056-1,060	746.90	684.70	871.50
1,061-1,065	748.50	686.20	873.20
1,066-1,070	750.20	687.70	875.30
1,071-1,075	751.80	689.20	877.00
1,076-1,080	753.30	690.60	879.00
1,081-1,085	755.00	692.10	880.90
1,086-1,090	756.60	693.60	882.80
1,091-1,095	758.30	695.10	884.70
1,096-1,100	759.90	696.60	886.60
1,101-1,105	761.40	698.00	888.40
1,106-1,110	763.10	699.50	890.30
1,111-1,115	764.70	701.00	892.20
1,116-1,120	766.40	702.60	894.10
1,121-1,125	768.00	704.00	896.00
1,126-1,130	769.50	705.40	898.00
1,131-1,135	771.20	707.00	899.70
1,136-1,140	772.80	708.40	901.60
1,141-1,145	774.50	710.00	903.50
1,146-1,150	776.10	711.50	905.40
1,151-1,155	777.60	712.80	907.20
1,156-1,160	779.30	714.40	909.30
1,161-1,165	780.90	715.90	911.00
1,166-1,170	782.60	717.40	913.10
1,171-1,175	784.20	718.90	914.80

Checklist of Family Affairs

Name_____

Address_____

Phone: Home_____Business_____

This is an inventory of important and valuable papers and information, made on_____

_____19_____. Duplicate copies are in_____

and_____.

• My last will is kept_____. It was dated_____.

• I have a safe deposit box at_____. Box number_____.

People whose signatures authorize them to enter the box:
(names and addresses)

_____

_____

_____

The key is located_____.

There is a list of the contents_____.

These people are to be notified in the event of an emergency. They have my complete confidence and trust, and would know what to do, acting in the best interests of my family:

Name (and relationship)_____

Address_____

Name (and relationship)_____

Address_____

Following is a list of the key advisers for my family personal affairs. These people are familiar with my financial activities and with the members of my family, unless otherwise indicated:

Adviser	Name	Firm & Address	Phone
Executor(s) of will			
Attorney			
Banker			
Trust officer			
Insurance advisers and/or agents			
Accountant			
Tax consultant			
Broker(s)			
Business partner(s)			
Doctor(s)			
Clergymen			
Other			

The members of my family are (include all immediate relatives in direct line; relatives by marriage to direct descendants and predecessors; all others who may figure in your estate and the caring for your family after your death):

Name	Relationship to you	Address	Marital status	Birth date

Location of Personal Papers (your own, and family's)

What they are   *Where they are kept*

Certificates: Marriage

           Birth

           Baptismal

Wills: Your own (original and copies)

    By other members of your family

Military service records:

Social Security cards and numbers:

Employment records:

Organizations: Fraternal

           Unions

           Other

Automobile registration (number and
  renewal date):

Education records (report cards,
  transcripts):

Medical and health records (vaccinations,
  allergies, specific medication
  requirements, history):

Burial lot information:

Adoption papers:

Divorce or separation papers:

Passports:

Citizenship papers:

Other:

These are my family's *checking and savings accounts* (include banks, savings & loans, credit unions)

Name of firm	Address	Name account is in	Account number	Location of pass-book statements, canceled checks, etc.

These are the *U.S. savings bonds* owned by my family

Serial number	Names registered in, and beneficiary	Date purchased	Purchase price	Maturity date	Maturity value	Location

Commercial stocks, bonds, and other securities in the family

Company	Owner	Serial numbers	Date purchased	Number of shares	Cost per share	Location

Motor vehicles in the family (cars and/or trucks)

Who owns it	Make, model, year	Engine or serial no.	Purchase price	Loan(s) Amount	Lender	Location of records

Real estate owned (include records of cemetery plot)

Description and location	Date purchased	Purchase price	Mortgage or Contract Amount	Holder	Title in whose name	Location of records

Other business and property records (miscellaneous, except insurance)

Papers	Where they are kept
Tax returns, records, receipts (federal, state, and local):	
Real estate tax records and receipts (including home improvement over the years):	
Other tax records and receipts:	
Household inventory (item-by-item list of your home's contents, dates purchased, prices for major items; same for vacation homes, etc.):	
Special possessions (jewelry, electronic and photographic equipment, collections, furs, etc.—anything likely to be specially insured):	
Credit cards and charge accounts:	
Home accounting book:	
Receipts and sales slips:	

Papers	Where they are kept
Instructions, guarantees, and warranties on appliances:	
Property: Deeds	
Where deed recorded	
Abstracts of titles	
Business information (contracts, leases, partnership papers, etc.; names of associates, landlord):	
Rental information on second homes, other real estate:	
Information on trust instruments:	
Retirement papers (plans, information on pensions, etc.):	
Records kept for others:	
Keys:	
Other:	

I have these health, accident, and income protection policies

Company, agent, and address	Policy number	Name of insured	Date purchased	Expiration date

I have these life insurance policies

Company, agent, and address	Policy number	Who is insured/ policy owner	Face value	Beneficiary

Kind of insurance	Benefits	Premium		Where policy is kept
		Amount	Date due	

Type of policy	Cash or loan value	Premium		Where policy is kept
		Amount	Date due	

I have these policies on my house, car, and other property

Company, agent, and address	Policy number	Property insured and location	Amount of insurance	Dates of coverage

My insurance premiums are due on these dates

Policy Number Type	Jan.	Feb.	Mar.	Apr.	May	June	July	Aug.	Sept.	Oct.	Nov.	Dec.

Kind of insurance	Benefits	Premium		Where policy is kept
		Amount	Date due	

We owe these debts

Amount	Nature of debt	Owed by whom (name and address)	Payment plan	Final payment due	Where records are kept

These debts are owed to us

Amount	Nature of debt	Owed by whom (name and address)	Payment plan	Final payment due	Where records are kept

Index